C-1885   CAREER EXAMINATION SERIES

This is your
PASSBOOK for...

Mental Hygiene Treatment Team Leader

Test Preparation Study Guide
Questions & Answers

COPYRIGHT NOTICE

This book is SOLELY intended for, is sold ONLY to, and its use is RESTRICTED to individual, bona fide applicants or candidates who qualify by virtue of having seriously filed applications for appropriate license, certificate, professional and/or promotional advancement, higher school matriculation, scholarship, or other legitimate requirements of education and/or governmental authorities.

This book is NOT intended for use, class instruction, tutoring, training, duplication, copying, reprinting, excerption, or adaptation, etc., by:

1) Other publishers
2) Proprietors and/or Instructors of "Coaching" and/or Preparatory Courses
3) Personnel and/or Training Divisions of commercial, industrial, and governmental organizations
4) Schools, colleges, or universities and/or their departments and staffs, including teachers and other personnel
5) Testing Agencies or Bureaus
6) Study groups which seek by the purchase of a single volume to copy and/or duplicate and/or adapt this material for use by the group as a whole without having purchased individual volumes for each of the members of the group
7) Et al.

Such persons would be in violation of appropriate Federal and State statutes.

PROVISION OF LICENSING AGREEMENTS – Recognized educational, commercial, industrial, and governmental institutions and organizations, and others legitimately engaged in educational pursuits, including training, testing, and measurement activities, may address request for a licensing agreement to the copyright owners, who will determine whether, and under what conditions, including fees and charges, the materials in this book may be used them. In other words, a licensing facility exists for the legitimate use of the material in this book on other than an individual basis. However, it is asseverated and affirmed here that the material in this book CANNOT be used without the receipt of the express permission of such a licensing agreement from the Publishers. Inquiries re licensing should be addressed to the company, attention rights and permissions department.

All rights reserved, including the right of reproduction in whole or in part, in any form or by any means, electronic or mechanical, including photocopying, recording, or by any information storage and retrieval system, without permission in writing from the Publisher.

Copyright © 2025 by
National Learning Corporation

212 Michael Drive, Syosset, NY 11791
(516) 921-8888 • www.passbooks.com
E-mail: info@passbooks.com

PASSBOOK® SERIES

THE *PASSBOOK® SERIES* has been created to prepare applicants and candidates for the ultimate academic battlefield – the examination room.

At some time in our lives, each and every one of us may be required to take an examination – for validation, matriculation, admission, qualification, registration, certification, or licensure.

Based on the assumption that every applicant or candidate has met the basic formal educational standards, has taken the required number of courses, and read the necessary texts, the *PASSBOOK® SERIES* furnishes the one special preparation which may assure passing with confidence, instead of failing with insecurity. Examination questions – together with answers – are furnished as the basic vehicle for study so that the mysteries of the examination and its compounding difficulties may be eliminated or diminished by a sure method.

This book is meant to help you pass your examination provided that you qualify and are serious in your objective.

The entire field is reviewed through the huge store of content information which is succinctly presented through a provocative and challenging approach – the question-and-answer method.

A climate of success is established by furnishing the correct answers at the end of each test.

You soon learn to recognize types of questions, forms of questions, and patterns of questioning. You may even begin to anticipate expected outcomes.

You perceive that many questions are repeated or adapted so that you can gain acute insights, which may enable you to score many sure points.

You learn how to confront new questions, or types of questions, and to attack them confidently and work out the correct answers.

You note objectives and emphases, and recognize pitfalls and dangers, so that you may make positive educational adjustments.

Moreover, you are kept fully informed in relation to new concepts, methods, practices, and directions in the field.

You discover that you are actually taking the examination all the time: you are preparing for the examination by "taking" an examination, not by reading extraneous and/or supererogatory textbooks.

In short, this PASSBOOK®, used directedly, should be an important factor in helping you to pass your test.

MENTAL HYGIENE TREATMENT TEAM LEADER

DUTIES
Under the direct supervision of a Chief of Service (medical or non-medical), a Treatment Team Leader plans, organizes and supervises the implementation of a residential, habilitation, clinical, day center or community program for mentally ill, mentally disabled or developmentally disabled persons. The Treatment Team Leader has program and administrative responsibility for the treatment activities of an interdisciplinary treatment team and directs and coordinates a total program tailored to the individual needs of clients. The Team Leader will be responsible for marshalling and assigning team resources to accomplish team goals and evaluates the team's programs. The treatment team works in a variety of settings, both within and outside the facility.

SCOPE OF THE EXAMINATION
The <u>multiple-choice</u> test will cover knowledge, skills and abilities in such areas as:

1. Characteristics and treatment needs of individuals with mental disabilities and/or developmental disabilities;
2. Characteristics and treatment needs of individuals with mental illness;
3. Preparing written material; and
4. Issues, problems and situations encountered in the administration of treatment services.

INTRODUCTION

The written test for the Treatment Team Leader series has a time allowance of five hours. The test will cover the following subject areas:

1. **Characteristics and treatment needs of individuals with mental retardation and/or developmental disabilities:** These questions will test your knowledge of the characteristics and treatment needs of children, youth, adults and elderly who are receiving services from the Office of Mental Retardation and Developmental Disabilities, and your ability to recognize the signs, symptoms and etiology of mental retardation and/or developmental disabilities. *(Examination 36-145 only)*

2. **Characteristics and treatment needs of individuals with mental illness:** These questions will test your knowledge of the characteristics and treatment needs of children, youth, adults, and elderly who are receiving services from the Office of Mental Health, and your ability to recognize the signs, symptoms, and etiology of mental illness. *(Examinations 36-141, 36-142, 36-143, and 36-144 only)*

3. **Preparing written material:** These questions test for the ability to present information clearly and accurately, and to organize paragraphs logically and comprehensibly. For some questions, you will be given information in two or three sentences, followed by four restatements of the information. You must then choose the best version. For other questions, you will be given paragraphs with their sentences out of order. You must then choose, from among four choices, the best order for the sentences. *(All examinations)*

4. **Issues, problems and situations encountered in the administration of treatment services:** This subtest will test for the ability to deal with issues, problems, and situations associated with the administration, management, supervision, and provision of treatment services, using your analytical, organizational, interpersonal, judgment, decision-making, and communication skills. *(All examinations)*

The remainder of this test guide explains how you will be tested in each of the subject areas listed above. A **Test Task** is provided for each subject area. This is an explanation of how a question will be presented and how to correctly answer it. Read each explanation carefully. This test guide provides at least one **Sample Question** for each subject area. The sample questions will be similar to what will be presented on the actual test. The sample job simulation exercise section will be similar to what will be presented on the actual test. This test guide provides the **Solution** and correct answer(s) to each sample question. You should study these in order to understand how the correct or best answers were determined.

SUBJECT AREA 1

Characteristics and treatment needs of individuals with mental retardation and/or developmental disabilities: These questions will test your knowledge of the characteristics and treatment needs of children, youth, adults and elderly who are receiving services from the Office of Mental Retardation and Developmental Disabilities, and your ability to recognize the signs, symptoms and etiology of mental retardation and/or developmental disabilities.

There will be 15 questions in this subject area on the written test.

Test Task: You will be presented with situations in which you must apply your knowledge of the characteristics and treatment needs of clients who are diagnosed with mental retardation and/or developmental disabilities.

SAMPLE QUESTION:

A case worker has been working with a mentally retarded client for some months, and the client has become very dependent. The client calls the case worker nearly every day, sometimes many times a day, to ask for advice on ordinary decisions such as food selection during grocery shopping. These phone calls frequently interrupt the case worker's sessions with other clients. Which one of the following describes the BEST approach for the case worker to take in handling this problem?

A. Have an office secretary or staff person field the phone calls.
B. Assign the client to another case worker.
C. Set up an agreement with the client setting a specific time of the day when you will accept phone calls.
D. Allow the phone calls to roll over to voice mail and answer them as time permits each day.

The best answer to this sample question is C.

Choice A is not correct. This response will not solve the client's dependency and may lead to frustration, resulting in an increased number of telephone calls.

Choice B is not correct. This response is transferring the problem to another worker instead of solving the problem.

Choice C is the correct answer to this question. This response will eventually change the problem behavior, and it will involve working with the client, rather than working around the client.

Choice D is not correct. This response allows the behavior to continue and does not involve confronting the client about the behavior.

SUBJECT AREA 2

Characteristics and treatment needs of individuals with mental illness: These questions will test your knowledge of the characteristics and treatment needs of children, youth, adults and elderly who are receiving services from the Office of Mental Health, and your ability to recognize the signs, symptoms and etiology of mental illness.

There will be 15 questions in this subject area on the written test.

Test Task: You will be presented with situations in which you must apply your knowledge of the characteristics and treatment needs of clients who are diagnosed with mental illness.

SAMPLE QUESTION:

Your new client has a diagnosis of Intermittent Explosive Disorder. Based on this information, you should expect the client to present which one of the following symptoms?

A. anxiety in groups or open areas
B. delusions of persecution
C. auditory hallucinations
D. impulses leading to aggressive behavior

The best answer to this sample question is D.

Choice A is not correct. This response refers to symptoms of a phobia such as agoraphobia

Choice B is not correct. This response refers to a common symptom of mania

Choice C is not correct. This response refers to a common symptom of psychotic disorders

Choice D is the correct response.

SUBJECT AREA 3

Preparing Written Material: These questions test for the ability to present information clearly and accurately, and to organize paragraphs logically and comprehensibly. For some questions, you will be given information in two or three sentences, followed by four restatements of the information. You must then choose the best version. For other questions, you will be given paragraphs with their sentences out of order. You must then choose, from among four choices, the best order for the sentences. There will be 15 questions in this subject area on the written test.

Test Task:

There are two separate test tasks in this subject area.

- For the first, **Information Presentation**, you will be given information in two or three sentences, followed by four restatements of the information. You must then choose the best version.
- For the second, **Paragraph Organization**, you will be given paragraphs with their sentences out of order, and then be asked to choose, from among four suggestions, the best order for the sentences.

INFORMATION PRESENTATION SAMPLE QUESTION:

Martin Wilson failed to take proper precautions. His failure to take proper precautions caused a personal injury accident.

Which one of the following best presents the information above?

A. Martin Wilson failed to take proper precautions that caused a personal injury accident.
B. Proper precautions, which Martin Wilson failed to take, caused a personal injury accident.
C. Martin Wilson's failure to take proper precautions caused a personal injury accident.
D. Martin Wilson, who failed to take proper precautions, was in a personal injury accident.

The best answer to this sample question is C.

SOLUTION:

Choice A conveys the incorrect impression that proper precautions caused a personal injury accident.

Choice B conveys the incorrect impression that proper precautions caused a personal injury accident.

Choice C best presents the original information: Martin Wilson failed to take proper precautions and this failure caused a personal injury accident.

Choice D states that Martin Wilson was in a personal injury accident. The original information states that Martin Wilson caused a personal injury accident, but it does not state that Martin Wilson was in a personal injury accident.

PARAGRAPH ORGANIZATION SAMPLE QUESTION:

The following question is based upon a group of sentences. The sentences are shown out of sequence, but when correctly arranged, they form a connected, well-organized paragraph. Read the sentences, and then answer the question about the best arrangement of these sentences.

1. Eventually, they piece all of this information together and make a choice.
2. Before actually deciding upon a human services job, people usually think about several possibilities.
3. They imagine themselves in different situations, and in so doing, they probably think about their interests, goals, and abilities.
4. Choosing among occupations in the field of human services is an important decision to make.

Which one of the following is the best arrangement of these sentences?

A. 2-4-1-3
B. 2-3-4-1
C. 4-2-1-3
D. 4-2-3-1

The best answer to this sample question is D.

SOLUTION:

Choices A and C *present the information in the paragraph out of logical sequence. In both A and C, sentence 1 comes before sentence 3. The key element in the organization of this paragraph is that sentence 3 contains the information to which sentence 1 refers; therefore, in logical sequence, sentence 3 should come before sentence 1.*

Choice B *also presents the information in the paragraph out of logical sequence. Choice B places sentence 4 in between sentence 1 and sentence 3, thereby interrupting the logical sequence of the information in the paragraph.*

Choice D *presents the information in the paragraph in the best logical sequence. Sentence 4 introduces the main idea of the paragraph: "choosing an occupation in the field of nutrition services." Sentences 2-3-1 then follow up on this idea by describing, in order, the steps involved in making such a choice. Choice* **D** *is the best answer to this sample question.*

SUBJECT AREA 4

Issues, problems, and situations encountered in the administration of treatment services: These questions will test for the ability to deal with issues, problems, and situations associated with the administration, management, supervision, and provision of treatment services, using your analytical, organizational, interpersonal, judgment, decision-making, and communication skills.

Test Task: In the job simulation exercises for this subject area, you will be presented with situations that test your ability to organize and prioritize work, oversee and control programs, analyze and solve problems related to clinical and administrative aspects of Treatment Team Leader work. There are two job simulation exercises, each in a separate booklet. All candidates must answer all of these questions.

The job simulation exercise will start with background information that tells you about the job setting and the programs, services and clients you will be working with. The Background may also include some job-related issues, situations, and/or resource materials for you to consider.

You will then be presented with a series of problems and situations that could be encountered by a Treatment Team Leader. Each situation will be followed by a list of choices that represent possible responses you could make in that situation. You are to read the information presented and select the best choice(s) to take to collect relevant information and/or resolve the problem(s) in the situation described.

Each job simulation will start with **Section A**. The sections will continue in alphabetical order to the end of the exercise. Each section will present you with choices, and you are to select the most appropriate choice(s) from among those presented.

Each section will tell you **how many** choices you may select in that section.
- Some sections will direct you to "**Choose ONLY ONE.**"
- Other sections will direct you to choose "**up to**" a specified number of choices. For example, for a section marked as "**Choose UP TO THREE.**" you may choose fewer than three if you wish, but you should **not** choose more than three.
- Some sections will direct you to "**Choose AS MANY as are appropriate.**"
- It is important that you **follow the directions to each section carefully.**

A choice can be positively or neutrally valued, depending on the appropriateness of that choice in the situation presented. Follow the instructions to each section carefully. Failure to follow the **Instructions for Marking Answer Choices** may result in a lower score.

In order to be scored, all your answers must be recorded on a separate, scannable answer sheet. You are to mark 'A' for the choices you select and 'B' for the choices you are not selecting.

The following instructions will appear at the end of each Section:

- Mark 'A' on your answer sheet if you are **selecting** that choice or action.
- Mark 'B' on your answer sheet if you are **not selecting** that choice or action.
- You must mark **A or B** for each choice presented.

You must mark either 'A' or 'B' for each choice presented because your answer sheet will be optically scanned by a machine that reads the darkest filled-in circle next to a choice number as your selection for that choice number. Marking 'A' for choices you select and 'B' for choices you do not select will ensure that your choices are recorded accurately.

For example, if you mark 'A' for Choice 1 and then decide to change your answer, you must completely erase the mark for 'A' *and* mark 'B' for Choice 1. If you only erase the mark for 'A', the scanner will still identify 'A' as your selection because it is the darkest "filled-in circle." If you erase the mark in 'A' and mark 'B' for Choice 1 instead, the scanner will identify answer 'B' as the darkest "filled-in circle." Do NOT leave any numbered choice blank.

Sample Job Simulation Exercise

BACKGROUND INFORMATION

Assume that you are a Treatment Team Leader and have responsibility for a Community Residence with ten individuals and three staff members. Some of the individuals residing in the residence are ambulatory and some are not.

Today is Monday, November 2, 2009. You are observing a cooking lesson given by one staff member with two ambulatory residents in the kitchen of the residence. A fire suddenly flares up at the stove.

Continue now with SECTION A on the next page.

SECTION A

You would now: (**Choose UP TO THREE.**)

1. Pull the fire alarm to alert residents.
2. Help remove the residents in the kitchen.
3. Telephone the fire department.
4. Dial 911 on the telephone.
5. Telephone the Central Office of your agency.
6. Walk through the residence looking for the other eight residents.
7. Go outside and check which residents have been evacuated.
8. Locate a fire extinguisher and fight the fire until the fire department arrives.

For the choices in this section:

- Mark 'A' on your answer sheet if you are **selecting** that choice or action.
- Mark 'B' on your answer sheet if you are **not selecting** that choice or action.
- You must mark **A or B** for each choice presented.

Then, go to SECTION B on the next page.

Solution to the Sample Job Simulation Exercise

In **Sample Section A**, the best actions to take are choices 1, 4, and 7. On the answer paper, these choices should be marked **A** to indicate you are selecting them. The other choices should be marked **B** to indicate you are **not** selecting them as correct answers.

Choices 1, 4, and 7 are correct. These actions will help to ensure the safety of the residents and staff by immediately informing residents and staff (by the alarm) that there is an emergency, by ensuring a fast response by the Fire Department, and by allowing you to monitor and coordinate evacuation efforts by staff.

Choice 2 is not correct. This is the job of the staff person who was giving the lesson, and the ratio of staff to resident suggests no assistance will be needed. Your job in this situation is to ensure the safety of residents and staff and to ensure that all needed steps are followed in this emergency.

Choice 3 is not correct. Calling 911 would automatically pinpoint the location of the house for emergency responders; calling the fire department requires you to give the address and location verbally, which could be misunderstood, delaying the arrival of emergency crews.

Choice 5 is not correct. At this point in time, you would not spend time on the phone with the Central Office for your agency. In this emergency situation, your first responsibility is to ensure the safety and well-being of the residents and staff.

Choice 6 is not correct. You need to allow staff to perform their assigned tasks. You would not know exactly which residents were home and which were off grounds for medical appointments or treatment without asking staff first. Also, you could be trapped looking for a resident who is currently off-site.

Choice 8 is not correct. It is not your job to fight the fire, and an incorrect action in this emergency could cause injury to yourself and to residents. Your job is more important—to ensure the safety of clients and staff.

Choices 2, 3, 5, 6, and 8 represent actions that are inappropriate or a waste of time. Those choices should be marked B to indicate you are not selecting them as correct answers.

EXAMPLE FOR MARKING YOUR ANSWER PAPER:

In the sample **Section A**, a section with instructions to **"Choose UP TO THREE,"** a candidate who selected the three correct choices (Choices 1, 4, and 7) would mark **"A"** for these choices, and would mark **"B"** for Choices 2, 3, 5, 6, and 8.

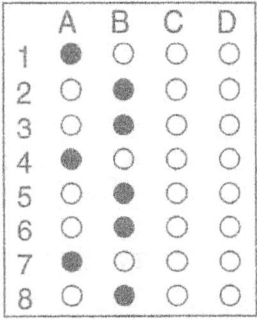

Solution to Section A

In the sample **Section A**, the most helpful steps to take in this emergency situation are those that ensure residents and staff are safely evacuated and accounted for, and that emergency responders arrive quickly to control the fire. **Choices 1, 4, and 7** are appropriate responses and are valued at +1.

Choices 2, 3, 5, 6, and 8 could hinder the evacuation, could slow response time by the emergency responders, or take up valuable time. These choices are each valued at + 0.

Listed below are all the choices presented in sample **Section A** and their assigned values:

1. Pull the fire alarm to alert residents.   +1
2. Help remove the residents in the kitchen.   0
3. Telephone the fire department.   0
4. Dial 911 on the telephone.   +1
5. Telephone the Central Office of your agency.   0
6. Walk through the entire residence looking for the other eight residents.   0
7. Go outside and check which residents have been evacuated.   +1
8. Locate a fire extinguisher; fight the fire until the fire department arrives.   0

HOW TO TAKE A TEST

I. YOU MUST PASS AN EXAMINATION

A. WHAT EVERY CANDIDATE SHOULD KNOW

Examination applicants often ask us for help in preparing for the written test. What can I study in advance? What kinds of questions will be asked? How will the test be given? How will the papers be graded?

As an applicant for a civil service examination, you may be wondering about some of these things. Our purpose here is to suggest effective methods of advance study and to describe civil service examinations.

Your chances for success on this examination can be increased if you know how to prepare. Those "pre-examination jitters" can be reduced if you know what to expect. You can even experience an adventure in good citizenship if you know why civil service exams are given.

B. WHY ARE CIVIL SERVICE EXAMINATIONS GIVEN?

Civil service examinations are important to you in two ways. As a citizen, you want public jobs filled by employees who know how to do their work. As a job seeker, you want a fair chance to compete for that job on an equal footing with other candidates. The best-known means of accomplishing this two-fold goal is the competitive examination.

Exams are widely publicized throughout the nation. They may be administered for jobs in federal, state, city, municipal, town or village governments or agencies.

Any citizen may apply, with some limitations, such as the age or residence of applicants. Your experience and education may be reviewed to see whether you meet the requirements for the particular examination. When these requirements exist, they are reasonable and applied consistently to all applicants. Thus, a competitive examination may cause you some uneasiness now, but it is your privilege and safeguard.

C. HOW ARE CIVIL SERVICE EXAMS DEVELOPED?

Examinations are carefully written by trained technicians who are specialists in the field known as "psychological measurement," in consultation with recognized authorities in the field of work that the test will cover. These experts recommend the subject matter areas or skills to be tested; only those knowledges or skills important to your success on the job are included. The most reliable books and source materials available are used as references. Together, the experts and technicians judge the difficulty level of the questions.

Test technicians know how to phrase questions so that the problem is clearly stated. Their ethics do not permit "trick" or "catch" questions. Questions may have been tried out on sample groups, or subjected to statistical analysis, to determine their usefulness.

Written tests are often used in combination with performance tests, ratings of training and experience, and oral interviews. All of these measures combine to form the best-known means of finding the right person for the right job.

II. HOW TO PASS THE WRITTEN TEST

A. NATURE OF THE EXAMINATION

To prepare intelligently for civil service examinations, you should know how they differ from school examinations you have taken. In school you were assigned certain definite pages to read or subjects to cover. The examination questions were quite detailed and usually emphasized memory. Civil service exams, on the other hand, try to discover your present ability to perform the duties of a position, plus your potentiality to learn these duties. In other words, a civil service exam attempts to predict how successful you will be. Questions cover such a broad area that they cannot be as minute and detailed as school exam questions.

In the public service similar kinds of work, or positions, are grouped together in one "class." This process is known as *position-classification*. All the positions in a class are paid according to the salary range for that class. One class title covers all of these positions, and they are all tested by the same examination.

B. FOUR BASIC STEPS

1) Study the announcement

How, then, can you know what subjects to study? Our best answer is: "Learn as much as possible about the class of positions for which you've applied." The exam will test the knowledge, skills and abilities needed to do the work.

Your most valuable source of information about the position you want is the official exam announcement. This announcement lists the training and experience qualifications. Check these standards and apply only if you come reasonably close to meeting them.

The brief description of the position in the examination announcement offers some clues to the subjects which will be tested. Think about the job itself. Review the duties in your mind. Can you perform them, or are there some in which you are rusty? Fill in the blank spots in your preparation.

Many jurisdictions preview the written test in the exam announcement by including a section called "Knowledge and Abilities Required," "Scope of the Examination," or some similar heading. Here you will find out specifically what fields will be tested.

2) Review your own background

Once you learn in general what the position is all about, and what you need to know to do the work, ask yourself which subjects you already know fairly well and which need improvement. You may wonder whether to concentrate on improving your strong areas or on building some background in your fields of weakness. When the announcement has specified "some knowledge" or "considerable knowledge," or has used adjectives like "beginning principles of…" or "advanced … methods," you can get a clue as to the number and difficulty of questions to be asked in any given field. More questions, and hence broader coverage, would be included for those subjects which are more important in the work. Now weigh your strengths and weaknesses against the job requirements and prepare accordingly.

3) Determine the level of the position

Another way to tell how intensively you should prepare is to understand the level of the job for which you are applying. Is it the entering level? In other words, is this the position in which beginners in a field of work are hired? Or is it an intermediate or advanced level? Sometimes this is indicated by such words as "Junior" or "Senior" in the class title. Other jurisdictions use Roman numerals to designate the level – Clerk I, Clerk II, for example. The word "Supervisor" sometimes appears in the title. If the level is not indicated by the title, check the description of duties. Will you be working under very close supervision, or will you have responsibility for independent decisions in this work?

4) Choose appropriate study materials

Now that you know the subjects to be examined and the relative amount of each subject to be covered, you can choose suitable study materials. For beginning level jobs, or even advanced ones, if you have a pronounced weakness in some aspect of your training, read a modern, standard textbook in that field. Be sure it is up to date and has general coverage. Such books are normally available at your library, and the librarian will be glad to help you locate one. For entry-level positions, questions of appropriate difficulty are chosen – neither highly advanced questions, nor those too simple. Such questions require careful thought but not advanced training.

If the position for which you are applying is technical or advanced, you will read more advanced, specialized material. If you are already familiar with the basic principles of your field, elementary textbooks would waste your time. Concentrate on advanced textbooks and technical periodicals. Think through the concepts and review difficult problems in your field.

These are all general sources. You can get more ideas on your own initiative, following these leads. For example, training manuals and publications of the government agency which employs workers in your field can be useful, particularly for technical and professional positions. A letter or visit to the government department involved may result in more specific study suggestions, and certainly will provide you with a more definite idea of the exact nature of the position you are seeking.

III. KINDS OF TESTS

Tests are used for purposes other than measuring knowledge and ability to perform specified duties. For some positions, it is equally important to test ability to make adjustments to new situations or to profit from training. In others, basic mental abilities not dependent on information are essential. Questions which test these things may not appear as pertinent to the duties of the position as those which test for knowledge and information. Yet they are often highly important parts of a fair examination. For very general questions, it is almost impossible to help you direct your study efforts. What we can do is to point out some of the more common of these general abilities needed in public service positions and describe some typical questions.

1) General information

Broad, general information has been found useful for predicting job success in some kinds of work. This is tested in a variety of ways, from vocabulary lists to questions about current events. Basic background in some field of work, such as sociology or economics, may be sampled in a group of questions. Often these are principles which have become familiar to most persons through exposure rather than through formal training. It is difficult to advise you how to study for these questions; being alert to the world around you is our best suggestion.

2) Verbal ability

An example of an ability needed in many positions is verbal or language ability. Verbal ability is, in brief, the ability to use and understand words. Vocabulary and grammar tests are typical measures of this ability. Reading comprehension or paragraph interpretation questions are common in many kinds of civil service tests. You are given a paragraph of written material and asked to find its central meaning.

3) Numerical ability

Number skills can be tested by the familiar arithmetic problem, by checking paired lists of numbers to see which are alike and which are different, or by interpreting charts and graphs. In the latter test, a graph may be printed in the test booklet which you are asked to use as the basis for answering questions.

4) Observation

A popular test for law-enforcement positions is the observation test. A picture is shown to you for several minutes, then taken away. Questions about the picture test your ability to observe both details and larger elements.

5) Following directions

In many positions in the public service, the employee must be able to carry out written instructions dependably and accurately. You may be given a chart with several columns, each column listing a variety of information. The questions require you to carry out directions involving the information given in the chart.

6) Skills and aptitudes

Performance tests effectively measure some manual skills and aptitudes. When the skill is one in which you are trained, such as typing or shorthand, you can practice. These tests are often very much like those given in business school or high school courses. For many of the other skills and aptitudes, however, no short-time preparation can be made. Skills and abilities natural to you or that you have developed throughout your lifetime are being tested.

Many of the general questions just described provide all the data needed to answer the questions and ask you to use your reasoning ability to find the answers. Your best preparation for these tests, as well as for tests of facts and ideas, is to be at your physical and mental best. You, no doubt, have your own methods of getting into an exam-taking mood and keeping "in shape." The next section lists some ideas on this subject.

IV. KINDS OF QUESTIONS

Only rarely is the "essay" question, which you answer in narrative form, used in civil service tests. Civil service tests are usually of the short-answer type. Full instructions for answering these questions will be given to you at the examination. But in case this is your first experience with short-answer questions and separate answer sheets, here is what you need to know:

1) Multiple-choice Questions

Most popular of the short-answer questions is the "multiple choice" or "best answer" question. It can be used, for example, to test for factual knowledge, ability to solve problems or judgment in meeting situations found at work.

A multiple-choice question is normally one of three types—
- It can begin with an incomplete statement followed by several possible endings. You are to find the one ending which *best* completes the statement, although some of the others may not be entirely wrong.
- It can also be a complete statement in the form of a question which is answered by choosing one of the statements listed.

- It can be in the form of a problem – again you select the best answer.

Here is an example of a multiple-choice question with a discussion which should give you some clues as to the method for choosing the right answer:

When an employee has a complaint about his assignment, the action which will *best* help him overcome his difficulty is to
- A. discuss his difficulty with his coworkers
- B. take the problem to the head of the organization
- C. take the problem to the person who gave him the assignment
- D. say nothing to anyone about his complaint

In answering this question, you should study each of the choices to find which is best. Consider choice "A" – Certainly an employee may discuss his complaint with fellow employees, but no change or improvement can result, and the complaint remains unresolved. Choice "B" is a poor choice since the head of the organization probably does not know what assignment you have been given, and taking your problem to him is known as "going over the head" of the supervisor. The supervisor, or person who made the assignment, is the person who can clarify it or correct any injustice. Choice "C" is, therefore, correct. To say nothing, as in choice "D," is unwise. Supervisors have and interest in knowing the problems employees are facing, and the employee is seeking a solution to his problem.

2) True/False Questions

The "true/false" or "right/wrong" form of question is sometimes used. Here a complete statement is given. Your job is to decide whether the statement is right or wrong.

SAMPLE: A roaming cell-phone call to a nearby city costs less than a non-roaming call to a distant city.

This statement is wrong, or false, since roaming calls are more expensive.

This is not a complete list of all possible question forms, although most of the others are variations of these common types. You will always get complete directions for answering questions. Be sure you understand *how* to mark your answers – ask questions until you do.

V. RECORDING YOUR ANSWERS

Computer terminals are used more and more today for many different kinds of exams.
For an examination with very few applicants, you may be told to record your answers in the test booklet itself. Separate answer sheets are much more common. If this separate answer sheet is to be scored by machine – and this is often the case – it is highly important that you mark your answers correctly in order to get credit.

An electronic scoring machine is often used in civil service offices because of the speed with which papers can be scored. Machine-scored answer sheets must be marked with a pencil, which will be given to you. This pencil has a high graphite content which responds to the electronic scoring machine. As a matter of fact, stray dots may register as answers, so do not let your pencil rest on the answer sheet while you are pondering the correct answer. Also, if your pencil lead breaks or is otherwise defective, ask for another.

Since the answer sheet will be dropped in a slot in the scoring machine, be careful not to bend the corners or get the paper crumpled.

The answer sheet normally has five vertical columns of numbers, with 30 numbers to a column. These numbers correspond to the question numbers in your test booklet. After each number, going across the page are four or five pairs of dotted lines. These short dotted lines have small letters or numbers above them. The first two pairs may also have a "T" or "F" above the letters. This indicates that the first two pairs only are to be used if the questions are of the true-false type. If the questions are multiple choice, disregard the "T" and "F" and pay attention only to the small letters or numbers.

Answer your questions in the manner of the sample that follows:

32. The largest city in the United States is
    A. Washington, D.C.
    B. New York City
    C. Chicago
    D. Detroit
    E. San Francisco

1) Choose the answer you think is best. (New York City is the largest, so "B" is correct.)
2) Find the row of dotted lines numbered the same as the question you are answering. (Find row number 32)
3) Find the pair of dotted lines corresponding to the answer. (Find the pair of lines under the mark "B.")
4) Make a solid black mark between the dotted lines.

VI. BEFORE THE TEST

Common sense will help you find procedures to follow to get ready for an examination. Too many of us, however, overlook these sensible measures. Indeed, nervousness and fatigue have been found to be the most serious reasons why applicants fail to do their best on civil service tests. Here is a list of reminders:

- Begin your preparation early – Don't wait until the last minute to go scurrying around for books and materials or to find out what the position is all about.
- Prepare continuously – An hour a night for a week is better than an all-night cram session. This has been definitely established. What is more, a night a week for a month will return better dividends than crowding your study into a shorter period of time.
- Locate the place of the exam – You have been sent a notice telling you when and where to report for the examination. If the location is in a different town or otherwise unfamiliar to you, it would be well to inquire the best route and learn something about the building.
- Relax the night before the test – Allow your mind to rest. Do not study at all that night. Plan some mild recreation or diversion; then go to bed early and get a good night's sleep.
- Get up early enough to make a leisurely trip to the place for the test – This way unforeseen events, traffic snarls, unfamiliar buildings, etc. will not upset you.
- Dress comfortably – A written test is not a fashion show. You will be known by number and not by name, so wear something comfortable.

- Leave excess paraphernalia at home – Shopping bags and odd bundles will get in your way. You need bring only the items mentioned in the official notice you received; usually everything you need is provided. Do not bring reference books to the exam. They will only confuse those last minutes and be taken away from you when in the test room.
- Arrive somewhat ahead of time – If because of transportation schedules you must get there very early, bring a newspaper or magazine to take your mind off yourself while waiting.
- Locate the examination room – When you have found the proper room, you will be directed to the seat or part of the room where you will sit. Sometimes you are given a sheet of instructions to read while you are waiting. Do not fill out any forms until you are told to do so; just read them and be prepared.
- Relax and prepare to listen to the instructions
- If you have any physical problem that may keep you from doing your best, be sure to tell the test administrator. If you are sick or in poor health, you really cannot do your best on the exam. You can come back and take the test some other time.

VII. AT THE TEST

The day of the test is here and you have the test booklet in your hand. The temptation to get going is very strong. Caution! There is more to success than knowing the right answers. You must know how to identify your papers and understand variations in the type of short-answer question used in this particular examination. Follow these suggestions for maximum results from your efforts:

1) Cooperate with the monitor

The test administrator has a duty to create a situation in which you can be as much at ease as possible. He will give instructions, tell you when to begin, check to see that you are marking your answer sheet correctly, and so on. He is not there to guard you, although he will see that your competitors do not take unfair advantage. He wants to help you do your best.

2) Listen to all instructions

Don't jump the gun! Wait until you understand all directions. In most civil service tests you get more time than you need to answer the questions. So don't be in a hurry. Read each word of instructions until you clearly understand the meaning. Study the examples, listen to all announcements and follow directions. Ask questions if you do not understand what to do.

3) Identify your papers

Civil service exams are usually identified by number only. You will be assigned a number; you must not put your name on your test papers. Be sure to copy your number correctly. Since more than one exam may be given, copy your exact examination title.

4) Plan your time

Unless you are told that a test is a "speed" or "rate of work" test, speed itself is usually not important. Time enough to answer all the questions will be provided, but this does not mean that you have all day. An overall time limit has been set. Divide the total time (in minutes) by the number of questions to determine the approximate time you have for each question.

5) Do not linger over difficult questions

If you come across a difficult question, mark it with a paper clip (useful to have along) and come back to it when you have been through the booklet. One caution if you do this – be sure to skip a number on your answer sheet as well. Check often to be sure that you have not lost your place and that you are marking in the row numbered the same as the question you are answering.

6) Read the questions

Be sure you know what the question asks! Many capable people are unsuccessful because they failed to *read* the questions correctly.

7) Answer all questions

Unless you have been instructed that a penalty will be deducted for incorrect answers, it is better to guess than to omit a question.

8) Speed tests

It is often better NOT to guess on speed tests. It has been found that on timed tests people are tempted to spend the last few seconds before time is called in marking answers at random – without even reading them – in the hope of picking up a few extra points. To discourage this practice, the instructions may warn you that your score will be "corrected" for guessing. That is, a penalty will be applied. The incorrect answers will be deducted from the correct ones, or some other penalty formula will be used.

9) Review your answers

If you finish before time is called, go back to the questions you guessed or omitted to give them further thought. Review other answers if you have time.

10) Return your test materials

If you are ready to leave before others have finished or time is called, take ALL your materials to the monitor and leave quietly. Never take any test material with you. The monitor can discover whose papers are not complete, and taking a test booklet may be grounds for disqualification.

VIII. EXAMINATION TECHNIQUES

1) Read the general instructions carefully. These are usually printed on the first page of the exam booklet. As a rule, these instructions refer to the timing of the examination; the fact that you should not start work until the signal and must stop work at a signal, etc. If there are any *special* instructions, such as a choice of questions to be answered, make sure that you note this instruction carefully.

2) When you are ready to start work on the examination, that is as soon as the signal has been given, read the instructions to each question booklet, underline any key words or phrases, such as *least, best, outline, describe* and the like. In this way you will tend to answer as requested rather than discover on reviewing your paper that you *listed without describing*, that you selected the *worst* choice rather than the *best* choice, etc.

3) If the examination is of the objective or multiple-choice type – that is, each question will also give a series of possible answers: A, B, C or D, and you are called upon to select the best answer and write the letter next to that answer on your answer paper – it is advisable to start answering each question in turn. There may be anywhere from 50 to 100 such questions in the three or four hours allotted and you can see how much time would be taken if you read through all the questions before beginning to answer any. Furthermore, if you come across a question or group of questions which you know would be difficult to answer, it would undoubtedly affect your handling of all the other questions.

4) If the examination is of the essay type and contains but a few questions, it is a moot point as to whether you should read all the questions before starting to answer any one. Of course, if you are given a choice – say five out of seven and the like – then it is essential to read all the questions so you can eliminate the two that are most difficult. If, however, you are asked to answer all the questions, there may be danger in trying to answer the easiest one first because you may find that you will spend too much time on it. The best technique is to answer the first question, then proceed to the second, etc.

5) Time your answers. Before the exam begins, write down the time it started, then add the time allowed for the examination and write down the time it must be completed, then divide the time available somewhat as follows:
   - If 3-1/2 hours are allowed, that would be 210 minutes. If you have 80 objective-type questions, that would be an average of 2-1/2 minutes per question. Allow yourself no more than 2 minutes per question, or a total of 160 minutes, which will permit about 50 minutes to review.
   - If for the time allotment of 210 minutes there are 7 essay questions to answer, that would average about 30 minutes a question. Give yourself only 25 minutes per question so that you have about 35 minutes to review.

6) The most important instruction is to *read each question* and make sure you know what is wanted. The second most important instruction is to *time yourself properly* so that you answer every question. The third most important instruction is to *answer every question*. Guess if you have to but include something for each question. Remember that you will receive no credit for a blank and will probably receive some credit if you write something in answer to an essay question. If you guess a letter – say "B" for a multiple-choice question – you may have guessed right. If you leave a blank as an answer to a multiple-choice question, the examiners may respect your feelings but it will not add a point to your score. Some exams may penalize you for wrong answers, so in such cases *only*, you may not want to guess unless you have some basis for your answer.

7) Suggestions
   a. Objective-type questions
      1. Examine the question booklet for proper sequence of pages and questions
      2. Read all instructions carefully
      3. Skip any question which seems too difficult; return to it after all other questions have been answered
      4. Apportion your time properly; do not spend too much time on any single question or group of questions

5. Note and underline key words – *all, most, fewest, least, best, worst, same, opposite*, etc.
6. Pay particular attention to negatives
7. Note unusual option, e.g., unduly long, short, complex, different or similar in content to the body of the question
8. Observe the use of "hedging" words – *probably, may, most likely*, etc.
9. Make sure that your answer is put next to the same number as the question
10. Do not second-guess unless you have good reason to believe the second answer is definitely more correct
11. Cross out original answer if you decide another answer is more accurate; do not erase until you are ready to hand your paper in
12. Answer all questions; guess unless instructed otherwise
13. Leave time for review

b. Essay questions
1. Read each question carefully
2. Determine exactly what is wanted. Underline key words or phrases.
3. Decide on outline or paragraph answer
4. Include many different points and elements unless asked to develop any one or two points or elements
5. Show impartiality by giving pros and cons unless directed to select one side only
6. Make and write down any assumptions you find necessary to answer the questions
7. Watch your English, grammar, punctuation and choice of words
8. Time your answers; don't crowd material

8) Answering the essay question

Most essay questions can be answered by framing the specific response around several key words or ideas. Here are a few such key words or ideas:

M's: manpower, materials, methods, money, management
P's: purpose, program, policy, plan, procedure, practice, problems, pitfalls, personnel, public relations

a. Six basic steps in handling problems:
1. Preliminary plan and background development
2. Collect information, data and facts
3. Analyze and interpret information, data and facts
4. Analyze and develop solutions as well as make recommendations
5. Prepare report and sell recommendations
6. Install recommendations and follow up effectiveness

b. Pitfalls to avoid
1. *Taking things for granted* – A statement of the situation does not necessarily imply that each of the elements is necessarily true; for example, a complaint may be invalid and biased so that all that can be taken for granted is that a complaint has been registered

2. *Considering only one side of a situation* – Wherever possible, indicate several alternatives and then point out the reasons you selected the best one
3. *Failing to indicate follow up* – Whenever your answer indicates action on your part, make certain that you will take proper follow-up action to see how successful your recommendations, procedures or actions turn out to be
4. *Taking too long in answering any single question* – Remember to time your answers properly

IX. AFTER THE TEST

Scoring procedures differ in detail among civil service jurisdictions although the general principles are the same. Whether the papers are hand-scored or graded by machine we have described, they are nearly always graded by number. That is, the person who marks the paper knows only the number – never the name – of the applicant. Not until all the papers have been graded will they be matched with names. If other tests, such as training and experience or oral interview ratings have been given, scores will be combined. Different parts of the examination usually have different weights. For example, the written test might count 60 percent of the final grade, and a rating of training and experience 40 percent. In many jurisdictions, veterans will have a certain number of points added to their grades.

After the final grade has been determined, the names are placed in grade order and an eligible list is established. There are various methods for resolving ties between those who get the same final grade – probably the most common is to place first the name of the person whose application was received first. Job offers are made from the eligible list in the order the names appear on it. You will be notified of your grade and your rank as soon as all these computations have been made. This will be done as rapidly as possible.

People who are found to meet the requirements in the announcement are called "eligibles." Their names are put on a list of eligible candidates. An eligible's chances of getting a job depend on how high he stands on this list and how fast agencies are filling jobs from the list.

When a job is to be filled from a list of eligibles, the agency asks for the names of people on the list of eligibles for that job. When the civil service commission receives this request, it sends to the agency the names of the three people highest on this list. Or, if the job to be filled has specialized requirements, the office sends the agency the names of the top three persons who meet these requirements from the general list.

The appointing officer makes a choice from among the three people whose names were sent to him. If the selected person accepts the appointment, the names of the others are put back on the list to be considered for future openings.

That is the rule in hiring from all kinds of eligible lists, whether they are for typist, carpenter, chemist, or something else. For every vacancy, the appointing officer has his choice of any one of the top three eligibles on the list. This explains why the person whose name is on top of the list sometimes does not get an appointment when some of the persons lower on the list do. If the appointing officer chooses the second or third eligible, the No. 1 eligible does not get a job at once, but stays on the list until he is appointed or the list is terminated.

X. HOW TO PASS THE INTERVIEW TEST

The examination for which you applied requires an oral interview test. You have already taken the written test and you are now being called for the interview test – the final part of the formal examination.

You may think that it is not possible to prepare for an interview test and that there are no procedures to follow during an interview. Our purpose is to point out some things you can do in advance that will help you and some good rules to follow and pitfalls to avoid while you are being interviewed.

What is an interview supposed to test?

The written examination is designed to test the technical knowledge and competence of the candidate; the oral is designed to evaluate intangible qualities, not readily measured otherwise, and to establish a list showing the relative fitness of each candidate – as measured against his competitors – for the position sought. Scoring is not on the basis of "right" and "wrong," but on a sliding scale of values ranging from "not passable" to "outstanding." As a matter of fact, it is possible to achieve a relatively low score without a single "incorrect" answer because of evident weakness in the qualities being measured.

Occasionally, an examination may consist entirely of an oral test – either an individual or a group oral. In such cases, information is sought concerning the technical knowledges and abilities of the candidate, since there has been no written examination for this purpose. More commonly, however, an oral test is used to supplement a written examination.

Who conducts interviews?

The composition of oral boards varies among different jurisdictions. In nearly all, a representative of the personnel department serves as chairman. One of the members of the board may be a representative of the department in which the candidate would work. In some cases, "outside experts" are used, and, frequently, a businessman or some other representative of the general public is asked to serve. Labor and management or other special groups may be represented. The aim is to secure the services of experts in the appropriate field.

However the board is composed, it is a good idea (and not at all improper or unethical) to ascertain in advance of the interview who the members are and what groups they represent. When you are introduced to them, you will have some idea of their backgrounds and interests, and at least you will not stutter and stammer over their names.

What should be done before the interview?

While knowledge about the board members is useful and takes some of the surprise element out of the interview, there is other preparation which is more substantive. It *is* possible to prepare for an oral interview – in several ways:

1) Keep a copy of your application and review it carefully before the interview

This may be the only document before the oral board, and the starting point of the interview. Know what education and experience you have listed there, and the sequence and dates of all of it. Sometimes the board will ask you to review the highlights of your experience for them; you should not have to hem and haw doing it.

2) Study the class specification and the examination announcement

Usually, the oral board has one or both of these to guide them. The qualities, characteristics or knowledges required by the position sought are stated in these documents. They offer valuable clues as to the nature of the oral interview. For example, if the job involves supervisory responsibilities, the announcement will usually indicate that knowledge of modern supervisory methods and the qualifications of the candidate as a supervisor will be tested. If so, you can expect such questions, frequently in the form of a hypothetical situation which you are expected to solve. NEVER go into an oral without knowledge of the duties and responsibilities of the job you seek.

3) Think through each qualification required

Try to visualize the kind of questions you would ask if you were a board member. How well could you answer them? Try especially to appraise your own knowledge and background in each area, *measured against the job sought*, and identify any areas in which you are weak. Be critical and realistic – do not flatter yourself.

4) Do some general reading in areas in which you feel you may be weak

For example, if the job involves supervision and your past experience has NOT, some general reading in supervisory methods and practices, particularly in the field of human relations, might be useful. Do NOT study agency procedures or detailed manuals. The oral board will be testing your understanding and capacity, not your memory.

5) Get a good night's sleep and watch your general health and mental attitude

You will want a clear head at the interview. Take care of a cold or any other minor ailment, and of course, no hangovers.

What should be done on the day of the interview?

Now comes the day of the interview itself. Give yourself plenty of time to get there. Plan to arrive somewhat ahead of the scheduled time, particularly if your appointment is in the fore part of the day. If a previous candidate fails to appear, the board might be ready for you a bit early. By early afternoon an oral board is almost invariably behind schedule if there are many candidates, and you may have to wait. Take along a book or magazine to read, or your application to review, but leave any extraneous material in the waiting room when you go in for your interview. In any event, relax and compose yourself.

The matter of dress is important. The board is forming impressions about you – from your experience, your manners, your attitude, and your appearance. Give your personal appearance careful attention. Dress your best, but not your flashiest. Choose conservative, appropriate clothing, and be sure it is immaculate. This is a business interview, and your appearance should indicate that you regard it as such. Besides, being well groomed and properly dressed will help boost your confidence.

Sooner or later, someone will call your name and escort you into the interview room. *This is it.* From here on you are on your own. It is too late for any more preparation. But remember, you asked for this opportunity to prove your fitness, and you are here because your request was granted.

What happens when you go in?

The usual sequence of events will be as follows: The clerk (who is often the board stenographer) will introduce you to the chairman of the oral board, who will introduce you to the other members of the board. Acknowledge the introductions before you sit down. Do not be surprised if you find a microphone facing you or a stenotypist sitting by. Oral interviews are usually recorded in the event of an appeal or other review.

Usually the chairman of the board will open the interview by reviewing the highlights of your education and work experience from your application – primarily for the benefit of the other members of the board, as well as to get the material into the record. Do not interrupt or comment unless there is an error or significant misinterpretation; if that is the case, do not hesitate. But do not quibble about insignificant matters. Also, he will usually ask you some question about your education, experience or your present job – partly to get you to start talking and to establish the interviewing "rapport." He may start the actual questioning, or turn it over to one of the other members. Frequently, each member undertakes the questioning on a particular area, one in which he is perhaps most competent, so you can expect each member to participate in the examination. Because time is limited, you may also expect some rather abrupt switches in the direction the questioning takes, so do not be upset by it. Normally, a board member will not pursue a single line of questioning unless he discovers a particular strength or weakness.

After each member has participated, the chairman will usually ask whether any member has any further questions, then will ask you if you have anything you wish to add. Unless you are expecting this question, it may floor you. Worse, it may start you off on an extended, extemporaneous speech. The board is not usually seeking more information. The question is principally to offer you a last opportunity to present further qualifications or to indicate that you have nothing to add. So, if you feel that a significant qualification or characteristic has been overlooked, it is proper to point it out in a sentence or so. Do not compliment the board on the thoroughness of their examination – they have been sketchy, and you know it. If you wish, merely say, "No thank you, I have nothing further to add." This is a point where you can "talk yourself out" of a good impression or fail to present an important bit of information. Remember, *you close the interview yourself.*

The chairman will then say, "That is all, Mr. _____, thank you." Do not be startled; the interview is over, and quicker than you think. Thank him, gather your belongings and take your leave. Save your sigh of relief for the other side of the door.

How to put your best foot forward
Throughout this entire process, you may feel that the board individually and collectively is trying to pierce your defenses, seek out your hidden weaknesses and embarrass and confuse you. Actually, this is not true. They are obliged to make an appraisal of your qualifications for the job you are seeking, and they want to see you in your best light. Remember, they must interview all candidates and a non-cooperative candidate may become a failure in spite of their best efforts to bring out his qualifications. Here are 15 suggestions that will help you:

1) Be natural – Keep your attitude confident, not cocky
If you are not confident that you can do the job, do not expect the board to be. Do not apologize for your weaknesses, try to bring out your strong points. The board is interested in a positive, not negative, presentation. Cockiness will antagonize any board member and make him wonder if you are covering up a weakness by a false show of strength.

2) Get comfortable, but don't lounge or sprawl
Sit erectly but not stiffly. A careless posture may lead the board to conclude that you are careless in other things, or at least that you are not impressed by the importance of the occasion. Either conclusion is natural, even if incorrect. Do not fuss with your clothing, a pencil or an ashtray. Your hands may occasionally be useful to emphasize a point; do not let them become a point of distraction.

3) Do not wisecrack or make small talk
This is a serious situation, and your attitude should show that you consider it as such. Further, the time of the board is limited – they do not want to waste it, and neither should you.

4) Do not exaggerate your experience or abilities

In the first place, from information in the application or other interviews and sources, the board may know more about you than you think. Secondly, you probably will not get away with it. An experienced board is rather adept at spotting such a situation, so do not take the chance.

5) If you know a board member, do not make a point of it, yet do not hide it

Certainly you are not fooling him, and probably not the other members of the board. Do not try to take advantage of your acquaintanceship – it will probably do you little good.

6) Do not dominate the interview

Let the board do that. They will give you the clues – do not assume that you have to do all the talking. Realize that the board has a number of questions to ask you, and do not try to take up all the interview time by showing off your extensive knowledge of the answer to the first one.

7) Be attentive

You only have 20 minutes or so, and you should keep your attention at its sharpest throughout. When a member is addressing a problem or question to you, give him your undivided attention. Address your reply principally to him, but do not exclude the other board members.

8) Do not interrupt

A board member may be stating a problem for you to analyze. He will ask you a question when the time comes. Let him state the problem, and wait for the question.

9) Make sure you understand the question

Do not try to answer until you are sure what the question is. If it is not clear, restate it in your own words or ask the board member to clarify it for you. However, do not haggle about minor elements.

10) Reply promptly but not hastily

A common entry on oral board rating sheets is "candidate responded readily," or "candidate hesitated in replies." Respond as promptly and quickly as you can, but do not jump to a hasty, ill-considered answer.

11) Do not be peremptory in your answers

A brief answer is proper – but do not fire your answer back. That is a losing game from your point of view. The board member can probably ask questions much faster than you can answer them.

12) Do not try to create the answer you think the board member wants

He is interested in what kind of mind you have and how it works – not in playing games. Furthermore, he can usually spot this practice and will actually grade you down on it.

13) Do not switch sides in your reply merely to agree with a board member

Frequently, a member will take a contrary position merely to draw you out and to see if you are willing and able to defend your point of view. Do not start a debate, yet do not surrender a good position. If a position is worth taking, it is worth defending.

14) Do not be afraid to admit an error in judgment if you are shown to be wrong

The board knows that you are forced to reply without any opportunity for careful consideration. Your answer may be demonstrably wrong. If so, admit it and get on with the interview.

15) Do not dwell at length on your present job

The opening question may relate to your present assignment. Answer the question but do not go into an extended discussion. You are being examined for a *new* job, not your present one. As a matter of fact, try to phrase ALL your answers in terms of the job for which you are being examined.

Basis of Rating

Probably you will forget most of these "do's" and "don'ts" when you walk into the oral interview room. Even remembering them all will not ensure you a passing grade. Perhaps you did not have the qualifications in the first place. But remembering them will help you to put your best foot forward, without treading on the toes of the board members.

Rumor and popular opinion to the contrary notwithstanding, an oral board wants you to make the best appearance possible. They know you are under pressure – but they also want to see how you respond to it as a guide to what your reaction would be under the pressures of the job you seek. They will be influenced by the degree of poise you display, the personal traits you show and the manner in which you respond.

ABOUT THIS BOOK

This book contains tests divided into Examination Sections. Go through each test, answering every question in the margin. We have also attached a sample answer sheet at the back of the book that can be removed and used. At the end of each test look at the answer key and check your answers. On the ones you got wrong, look at the right answer choice and learn. Do not fill in the answers first. Do not memorize the questions and answers, but understand the answer and principles involved. On your test, the questions will likely be different from the samples. Questions are changed and new ones added. If you understand these past questions you should have success with any changes that arise. Tests may consist of several types of questions. We have additional books on each subject should more study be advisable or necessary for you. Finally, the more you study, the better prepared you will be. This book is intended to be the last thing you study before you walk into the examination room. Prior study of relevant texts is also recommended. NLC publishes some of these in our Fundamental Series. Knowledge and good sense are important factors in passing your exam. Good luck also helps. So now study this Passbook, absorb the material contained within and take that knowledge into the examination. Then do your best to pass that exam.

EXAMINATION SECTION

EXAMINATION SECTION
TEST 1

DIRECTIONS: Each question or incomplete statement is followed by several suggested answers or completions. Select the one that BEST answers the question or completes the statement. *PRINT THE LETTER OF THE CORRECT ANSWER IN THE SPACE AT THE RIGHT.*

Questions 1-9.

DIRECTIONS: Questions 1 through 9 are to be answered on the basis of the following information.

Ms. Evelyn Hart, a 75-year-old widow, is admitted to a psychiatric hospital. Her son, who brings her, says that she has been confused and wandered away from home. Also, she has become increasingly careless about her appearance.

1. With a chronic brain syndrome such as Ms. Hart's, the personality changes are MOST often manifested as.

    A. an exaggeration of previous traits
    B. overt pleas for assistance
    C. suspicion and reticence
    D. marked resistance and negativism

2. During the early period following Ms. Hart's admission, the nursing procedure that would be BEST for her is

    A. carrying out activities in the same order each day
    B. insisting that she focus her conversation on present events
    C. providing a variety of novel experiences
    D. rotating staff assignments so that she will become acquainted with each member of the nursing staff

3. When Ms. Hart's son comes to visit her the day after admission, Ms. Hart refuses to talk to him. The son goes to the nurse and says, *My mother won't talk to me. Why is she acting like this? I had to do something with her. I couldn't keep her with us. Oh, what a mess!* Which of these responses by the nurse would be MOST appropriate initially?

    A. You feel guilty about having your mother here.
    B. Your mother is having a little difficulty adjusting to the hospital.
    C. This is a difficult situation for you and your mother.
    D. I'm sure you did the best you could under the circumstances.

4. Ms. Hart's son asks the nurse whether he should come to see his mother again on the following day in view of her reaction to his first visit.
Which of these responses would be BEST?

    A. Advising the son to wait until his mother gives some indication that she is ready to see him
    B. Suggesting that the son come back the next day since his continuing interest is important to his mother

1

C. Telling the son that his mother will not miss him if he doesn't visit because she will become attached to staff members
D. Informing the son that it is important for his mother to have visitors and suggesting that he ask one of her friends to visit her

5. The nurse finds Ms. Hart standing near the lavatory door. She has wet herself - as she does occasionally - because she does not allow herself sufficient time to reach the bathroom. Ms. Hart looks ashamed and turns her head away from the nurse.
Which of these responses by the nurse would be BEST?

    A. Asking, *Can you tell me why you wait so long, Ms. Hart?*
    B. Saying, *I know that this is upsetting to you, Ms. Hart. Come with me and I'll get a change of clothes for you*
    C. Asking, *Can you think of any way in which we can help you to manage your bathroom trips, Ms. Hart?*
    D. Sending Ms. Hart to her room to change her clothing

6. At about 3 P.M. one day, Ms. Hart comes to the nurse and says, *I haven't had a thing to eat all day.* The nurse knows that Ms. Hart did have lunch.
Which of these understandings by the nurse should be BASIC to a response?

    A. Confabulation is used by elderly patients as a means of relieving anxiety.
    B. Hunger is symbolic of a feeling of deprivation.
    C. Retrospective falsification is a mechanism commonly used by elderly persons who are unhappy.
    D. Loss of memory for recent events is characteristic of patients with senile dementia.

7. Ms. Hart is to be encouraged to increase her intake of protein.
The addition of which of these foods to 100 cc. of milk will provide the GREATEST amount of protein?

    A. 50 cc. light cream and 2 tablespoons corn syrup
    B. 30 grams powdered skim milk and 1 egg
    C. 1 small scoop (90 grams) vanilla ice cream and 1 tablespoon chocolate syrup
    D. 2 egg yolks and 1 tablespoon sugar

8. One day when another patient, Mr. Simon, is about to go to the canteen, Ms. Hart says to him, *Bring me a candy bar.* Mr. Simon replies, *Okay, give me the twenty-five cents for it.* Ms. Hart struggles with the idea, taking out a quarter and holding it but not giving it to Mr. Simon. Mr. Simon goes off impatiently, and Ms. Hart looks forlorn.
Which of these responses by the nurse would probably be MOST useful to Ms. Hart?

    A. *Ms. Hart, when we get things from the canteen, we have to pay for them. Do you want to buy candy?*
    B. *It was hard for you to decide whether or not to give Mr. Simon the money for the candy. Let's go to the canteen together.*
    C. *I know you are upset about Mr. Simon's going off, but he did have a right to ask you for the money for the candy.*
    D. *You feel you annoyed Mr. Simon. Would you like to talk about it?*

9. Ms. Hart tells stories over and over about her childhood. One day she keeps talking about holidays and how she used to make cookies for visiting children.
Which of the responses by the nurse would be BEST?

   A. That must have been a lot of fun, Ms. Hart. Will you help us make popcorn balls for the unit party?
   B. I can understand that those things were important to you, Ms. Hart. Now we can talk about something that is going on in the unit.
   C. Things are different now, Ms. Hart. What does your family serve as party refreshments nowadays?
   D. Those were the good old days. Did you ever go on a hayride?

Questions 10-17.

DIRECTIONS: Questions 10 through 17 are to be answered on the basis of the following information.

Mr. David Tripp, 28 years old, is brought from his place of work to the emergency department of a local general hospital by the police. He had been threatening his supervisor, who had criticized his work. During the admission procedure, he says, *They're all in on the plot to lock me up so I can't protect the world from them.*

10. During the early period of Mr. Tripp's hospitalization, which of these plans of care would probably be BEST for him?

    A. Encourage him to enter into simple group activities.
    B. Establish a daily routine that will help him become oriented to this new environment.
    C. Plan to cope with his slowness in carrying out his daily schedule.
    D. Assign the same members of the nursing team to care for him each day.

11. Mr. Tripp is on chlorpromazine hydrochloride (Thorazine) 100 mg. t.i.d. and 200 mg. at h.s.
The CHIEF purpose of chlorpromazine for Mr. Tripp is to

    A. relieve his anxiety
    B. control his aggression
    C. decrease his psychotic symptoms
    D. alleviate his depression

12. Mr. Tripp is walking into the dayroom when a male patient runs toward him screaming, *Let me out! Let me out!* A nurse's aide is following the screaming patient and is talking soothingly to him. Mr. Tripp seems panic-stricken and turns to flee.
Which of these initial responses to Mr. Tripp by the nurse would be BEST?

    A. Don't go, Mr. Tripp. That patient won't hurt you. He is frightened.
    B. It is upsetting to hear someone scream. The aide will help that patient. I will stay with you for a while, Mr. Tripp.
    C. Don't be upset, Mr. Tripp. That patient is sicker than you are. It's all right for you to go to your room if you like.
    D. This is nothing to be disturbed about, Mr. Tripp. It is part of that patient's illness.

13. One afternoon, Mr. Tripp is sitting in a small lounge watching a TV news program. During a biographical sketch of a criminal, Mr. Tripp begins to shout frantically, No, I am not one! You've no right to say that! Mr. Tripp's response to the program is MOST clearly an example of

    A. an idea of reference
    B. an obsession
    C. confabulation
    D. negativism

14. Mr. Tripp seems to value his regular sessions with the nurse, but on one occasion he becomes agitated and suddenly gets up and starts to mumble and pace back and forth. Which of these actions by the nurse would be BEST when Mr. Tripp does this?

    A. Sit quietly, while remaining attentive to him.
    B. Join him and pace with him.
    C. Leave the room until he calms down.
    D. Get a male nurse's aide to come and stand by and observe Mr. Tripp.

15. Mr. Tripp, who has read widely in the field of psychology, quotes fluently from various authorities with whose works the nurse is only vaguely acquainted.
    Which of these actions by the nurse in this situation would probably be BEST?

    A. Make an attempt to learn more about psychology in order to be able to converse with Mr. Tripp.
    B. Point out to Mr. Tripp that such theoretical knowledge is of little value unless it is applied in daily life.
    C. Listen attentively, in a relaxed manner, without attempting to compete with Mr. Tripp.
    D. Ask Mr. Tripp if he understands why he feels the need to give evidence of his knowledge of psychology.

16. Mr. Tripp is much improved and is to go home for a weekend. Since he is taking chlorpromazine hydrochloride (Thorazine), he should be given information regarding side-effects such as

    A. loss of pubic hair and weight gain
    B. agranulocytosis and nausea
    C. gastrointestinal bleeding and gynecomastia
    D. susceptibility to sunburn and potentation of alcohol

17. One day Mr. Tripp remarks to the nurse, Now that I can concentrate move, I can probably hold down a job when I'm discharged from the hospital.
    Which of these responses by the nurse would probably be MOST appropriate?

    A. Don't you expect to go back to your old job, Mr. Tripp?
    B. You have improved, Mr. Tripp, but you must be careful not to take on too much.
    C. Have you thought of something you might like to do, Mr. Tripp?
    D. There are agencies that will find work for you when you are ready, Mr. Tripp.

Questions 18-25.

DIRECTIONS: Questions 18 through 25 are to be answered on the basis of the following information.

Ms. Nancy Balm, a 20-year-old former music student, is admitted to a psychiatric hospital. Six months after entering school, she was dismissed for engaging in drug parties and sexual orgies in the dormitory. She has also been involved in the theft of a car and in several minor traffic violations. Ms. Balm has grown up in a permissive atmosphere with few controls.

18. After a few days, it is noted that Ms. Balm frequently seeks the attention of one of the female nurses; Ms. Balm calls her by her first name, offers to help her with her work, and frequently tells her that she is the nicest person on the unit.
Based on Ms. Balm's history, it is probably MOST justifiable to say that she

   A. has developed the capacity to be concerned about other people
   B. is asking for help from this nurse
   C. is attempting to use this nurse for her own purposes
   D. genuinely likes this nurse

19. Ms. Balm is on a locked unit. A new nurse on the unit is about to leave and is holding the key. Ms. Balm approaches, saying eagerly, *Let me turn the key and unlock the door. The other nurses let me.*
Which response by the nurse would be MOST appropriate?

   A. Going to the nurse in charge to ask if Ms. Balm's request should be granted
   B. Telling Ms. Balm in a friendly way that this is not permissible
   C. Letting Ms. Balm turn the key in the lock but keeping close to her while she does it
   D. Asking Ms. Balm why she feels that it is important for her to turn the key

20. One day Ms. Balm talks with the nurse about the events that led up to her hospitalization. She volunteers the information that she had stolen a car.
Considering the kind of illness she has, which additional comment that she might make would probably BEST indicate her basic attitude?

   A. I wanted a new sportscar, and that one was just what I had been looking for, so I took it.
   B. For a long time, I had wanted to steal a car but had been able to control my desire, but finally it overpowered me.
   C. I knew it was wrong to steal a car, but my friend dared me to.
   D. Once I had driven away in the car, I was sorry I had taken it.

21. At unit parties, Ms. Balm frequently dances with an elderly man who has chronic brain syndrome. She is courteous to him, though somewhat condescending. The elderly patient receives the attention happily.
It would be CORRECT for staff members to make which of these evaluations about this situation?

   A. Ms. Balm should not be permitted to dance with the elderly patient.
   B. Personnel should let Ms. Balm know that they are aware she is using this means to get approval.
   C. The elderly patient will terminate their relationship if he ceases to obtain pleasure from it.
   D. The activity need not be interrupted as long as both Ms. Balm and the elderly patient receive satisfaction from it.

22. A young male nurse who works with Ms. Balm has been going to the unit in the evening to see her. When questioned about this, the nurse states that he is fond of Ms. Balm. It would be ESSENTIAL for the nurse to recognize that

    A. his emotional involvement with Ms. Balm may interfere with his therapeutic effectiveness
    B. Ms. Balm's emotional involvement with him may interfere with her progress
    C. hospital policy prohibits romantic relationships between patients and nurses
    D. Ms. Balm may prove so demanding that he will drop the relationship, thus traumatizing her

23. When Ms. Balm's parents come to see her, they berate her for disgracing them, but they demand special privileges for her from the staff.
    It is probably MOST justified to say that they

    A. are unable to express their love directly to their daughter
    B. feel protective toward their daughter
    C. feel that a permissive environment would be better for their daughter
    D. have conflicting feelings about their daughter

24. Several patients are in the dayroom singing with a piano accompaniment. Ms. Balm enters and interrupts the group by turning on the television set. In addition to turning off the television set, which of these responses by the nurse would be MOST appropriate?

    A. Ask Ms. Balm if she would like to lead the group singing.
    B. Tell Ms. Balm that she cannot use the television while the group is singing and offer her a choice of some other activities.
    C. Tell Ms. Balm that she can watch television later.
    D. Tell Ms. Balm that she cannot stay in the dayroom if she continues to disturb the group.

25. Several weeks after Ms. Balm's admission, a group of patients who have written a play for a hospital party ask her to read the script because they know she had a story printed in the hospital newspaper. Ms. Balm agrees to do so and makes several good suggestions to the group, but does not try to assume control of the project.
    It is MOST justifiable to say that she is

    A. expressing a need to be liked
    B. indifferent to this project
    C. using a new method of manipulating the group
    D. showing improvement

KEY (CORRECT ANSWERS)

1. A
2. A
3. C
4. B
5. B

6. D
7. B
8. B
9. A
10. D

11. C
12. B
13. A
14. A
15. C

16. D
17. C
18. C
19. B
20. A

21. D
22. A
23. D
24. B
25. D

TEST 2

DIRECTIONS: Each question or incomplete statement is followed by several suggested answers or completions. Select the one that BEST answers the question or completes the statement. *PRINT THE LETTER OF THE CORRECT ANSWER IN THE SPACE AT THE RIGHT.*

Questions 1-9.

DIRECTIONS: Questions 1 through 9 are to be answered on the basis of the following information.

Andrew Miles, 18 years old and living away from home for the first time, is a freshman in college. He is admitted to the hospital because he has been having episodes in which he runs about, screams, and then drops to the floor and lies motionless for a few minutes, after which he gets up, mumbles *I'm sorry,* and behaves normally. His school record has been satisfactory, but his contacts with his peer group have decreased greatly because of these episodes. On the basis of diagnostic studies, it has been determined that Mr. Miles' illness is schizophrenia, catatonic type.

1. Stereotyped behavior such as that shown by Mr. Miles can be BEST explained as a(n)

    A. way of assuring predictability
    B. device to gain help and treatment
    C. means of increasing interpersonal distance
    D. attempt to control inner and outer forces

2. The behavior demonstrated by patients such as Mr. Miles is USUALLY thought to be indicative of

    A. damage to the cortex of the brain
    B. an expression of intrapersonal conflict
    C. a deficiency of vitamin B complex in the diet
    D. a disturbance in intellectual functioning

3. Upon Mr. Miles' admission, his needs would BEST be met by a plan that provides

    A. an introduction to each member of the staff
    B. a climate that makes few demands on him
    C. minimal sensory stimulation
    D. time for him to reflect on his problems without interference

4. The day after Mr. Miles' admission, a nurse, Ms. Caan, is assigned to stay with him for a period every day in order to establish a therapeutic nurse-patient relationship.
In carrying out this assignment, it is ESSENTIAL for this nurse to understand that Mr. Miles will probably

    A. be extremely sensitive to the feeling tones of others
    B. be unaware of the nurse's presence
    C. be hostile and verbally abusive
    D. talk if the nurse introduces topics that are of interest to him

5. Which of these insights that Mr. Miles might gain would be MOST basic to his improvement?

   A. Introjection of parental standards in childhood contributed to my personality.
   B. I am a person of worth and value.
   C. My behavior interferes with the development of good relationships.
   D. I require more reassurance than most people do.

6. One day a nurse finds Mr. Miles and another young male patient having an argument in the lounge. The other patient says, *Don't criticize me, you phony. You and your fits!* The other patient is pressing the argument, and Mr. Miles has run behind a chair.
   Which of these measures by the nurse would probably be BEST?

   A. Attempting to find out who started the argument
   B. Firmly directing each patient to go to his room
   C. Engaging the attention of the dominant patient
   D. Explaining to the other patient that Mr. Miles cannot control his spells

7. Mr. Miles now carries on brief conversations with Ms. Caan. During one such conversation, he seems relaxed and affable initially but soon begins to shift his position frequently, grasping the arms of his chair so tightly that his fingers blanch. Ms. Caan remarks to Mr. Miles that he seems tense, to which he replies *Yes.*
   Which of these responses by the nurse at this time would demonstrate the BEST understanding?

   A. I'm beginning to feel tense too, Mr. Miles.
   B. I wonder if I have said something wrong, Mr. Miles.
   C. Do women usually make you feel nervous, Mr. Miles.
   D. At what point in our talk did you begin to feel uneasy, Mr. Miles?

8. When Ms. Caan tells Mr. Miles that she will be off duty for two days, he says flatly, *So what. It doesn't matter.* It is MOST accurate to say that Mr. Miles is

   A. incapable of manifesting emotion
   B. confident of his ability to manage without the nurse
   C. controlling expression of his feelings
   D. apathetic toward the nurse

9. Family therapy is recommended for Mr. Miles. When explaining the purpose of this type of therapy to Mr. Miles' family, which of the following information would it be important to convey to them?

   A. Family members can reinforce the therapist's recommendations between sessions.
   B. Family members need advice in dealing with the identified patient's behavior.
   C. Joint treatment permits equal participation, eliminating anxieties that might otherwise lead to termination of treatment.
   D. Joint treatment alters family interaction, facilitating change in the behavior of the identified patient.

Questions 10-16.

DIRECTIONS: Questions 10 through 16 are to be answered on the basis of the following information.

Fifty-year-old Mr. Jack Dunn, accompanied by his wife, is brought to the emergency room by the police. He has been despondent because he was not promoted in his job. After calling his son to say goodbye, insisting that he was going to end it all, he locked himself in the bathroom, and the police were called to get him out. Mr. Dunn is admitted to the psychiatric unit.

10. Which of these interpretations of Mr. Dunn's behavior should serve as the basis for formulating his nursing care plan?
He

   A. wants to punish those around him
   B. is trying to manipulate his environment
   C. is attempting to get attention and sympathy
   D. is looking for relief from helplessness and hopelessness

11. Which of these statements ACCURATELY assesses Mr. Dunn's potential for suicide?
His

   A. sex and present stress suggest a high risk, but the likelihood of suicide is low in his age group
   B. threat suggests that the risk of suicide is minor
   C. age, sex, and present stress suggest a high risk of suicide
   D. sex suggests a low risk since suicide occurs 30 times more often in females than in males

12. Which of these occurrences would be MOST likely to result in an INCREASE in Mr. Dunn's suicidal thoughts?
His

   A. expressing hostility overtly before he is able to tolerate doing so
   B. entrance into a deeply retarded phase of depression
   C. being required to perform work in the kitchen
   D. being allowed to talk about his morbid ideas

13. During a staff conference concerning Mr. Dunn's care, a young nursing student says, *Even though I know that* Mr. Dunn's condition requires time to respond to therapy, I feel discouraged when I'm with him. No matter what I do, he talks about his failures and makes no attempt to help himself.
The interpretation of the student's reaction to Mr. Dunn's behavior that is probably MOST justifiable is that the

   A. student's difficulty arises from an attitude of hopelessness toward older persons
   B. student feels that Mr. Dunn's condition is not remediable unless he is willing to help himself
   C. student has set up a failure situation that is detrimental to therapeutic usefulness to Mr. Dunn
   D. student's self-concept as a helping person is being threatened

14. A nurse finds Mr. Dunn cutting his wrist with a razor blade.
Which of these actions should the nurse take?

   A. Shout *Stop!* and then say, *Tell me what caused your despair.*
   B. Say, *Think of what it would do to your family!*
   C. Grab Mr. Dunn's arm to stop him and say, *I'm going to stay with you.*
   D. Say, *Why, Mr. Dunn! You've just begun to feel better and now look what you've done.*

14.____

15. Mr. Dunn seems improved and is sent home on a trial visit. He is then admitted to the intensive care unit for treatment for a self-inflicted gunshot wound in the chest. When he is somewhat improved, Mr. Dunn remarks, *Everyone here must think I'm some kind of freak.*
Which of these responses would be MOST appropriate?

   A. None of us thinks that you are a freak.
   B. You feel that others are judging you.
   C. I understand that you were upset when this happened.
   D. What made you so desperate that you did a thing like this?

15.____

16. Mr. Dunn has improved and is discharged. A few days after Mr. Dunn returns to work, while he is talking with a co-worker, a number of things go wrong in the office. Mr. Dunn slams a book on the table and says, *Dammit!* The co-worker who is present is aware that Mr. Dunn has been mentally ill.
Which of these actions on the part of the co-worker would be BEST?

   A. Wait for Mr. Dunn to cool off and then resume the discussion.
   B. Suggest that Mr. Dunn go home and remain there until he calms down.
   C. Urge Mr. Dunn to take his tranquilizers.
   D. Talk with Mr. Dunn about his particular need for controlling outbursts.

16.____

Questions 17-25.

DIRECTIONS: Questions 17 through 25 are to be answered on the basis of the following information.

Ms. Julia Warren, 53 years old and with no previous history of mental illness, is admitted to a private psychiatric hospital because of symptoms, including pacing, wringing her hands, moaning, beating her forehead, and saying, *I'm a terrible woman.* She has been unable to do her job as a bookkeeper and has had to have members of her family stay with her day and night.

17. The extent of the nurse's orientation of Ms. Warren to the hospital environment should be based CHIEFLY upon Ms. Warren's

   A. willingness to stay with the nurse
   B. ability to concentrate
   C. persistence in making demands on other patients
   D. acceptance of the need for hospitalization

17.____

18. During the acute phase of Ms. Warren's illness, it is ESSENTIAL that the nurse have the ability to

    A. minimize stimuli in Ms. Warren's environment
    B. interest Ms. Warren in a variety of activities
    C. accept Ms. Warren's self-accusations
    D. strengthen Ms. Warren's intellectual defenses

19. Ms. Warren shows typical distress upon being informed of her impending electric convulsive therapy. Which understanding by the nurse would BEST serve as the basis for preparing Ms. Warren psychologically for it?

    A. Misinformation may be contributing to her anxiety.
    B. Emphasizing the safety of the procedure will reduce her fear.
    C. Knowing that most people have the same response is usually comforting.
    D. A high level of anxiety renders an individual more receptive to information given by helping persons.

20. Depressions of the type Ms. Warren has usually respond well to electric convulsive therapy, but the consequent memory loss is quite disturbing.
    The nurse can be MOST helpful to the patient who has such a loss of memory by

    A. engaging the patient in diversional activities
    B. reporting the problem to the physician
    C. explaining to the patient that other patients receiving this therapy also have this problem
    D. reassuring the patient repeatedly that this is an expected and temporary reaction

21. Which of the following defense mechanisms is MOST likely to be used by a person who is as depressed as Ms. Warren?

    A. Turning against the self
    B. Projection
    C. Rationalization
    D. Displacement of instinctual aims

22. When Ms. Warren learns that occupational therapy has been ordered for her, she scoffs at the idea, saying it is silly.
    If Ms. Warren were to think all of the following thoughts regarding occupational therapy, which one would be MOST acceptable to her?

    A. This is enjoyable.
    B. I'm helping to pay for my care.
    C. This keeps me from thinking about my failures.
    D. I didn't know that I was so creative,

23. Ms. Warren is assigned to group therapy. Which of these ideas would it be MOST desirable for each participant to gain?

    A. Each person's opinion is respected.
    B. Verbalization will help each individual to gain insight.
    C. Each member has a responsibility to other members of the group.
    D. The group work consists of analyzing each other's motivations.

24. Ms. Warren improves and goes out with her husband for the afternoon. That evening, a nurse finds Ms. Warren sitting by herself in the dayroom.
Which of these comments by the nurse would probably be BEST?

   A. Why are you so preoccupied, Ms. Warren?
   B. You look tired, Ms. Warren. Was your afternoon too much for you?
   C. You seem very quiet, Ms. Warren.
   D. You looked happier yesterday, Ms. Warren.

25. Ms. Warren is discharged. The day Ms. Warren goes back to work, Bob, a customer she has known for many years, comes in and says, *Hello there, Julia. Good to see you back! your boss told me that you were sick. What was wrong with you?* Which of these replies by Ms. Warren would indicate that she accepted her illness and has recovered?

   A. I was kind of mixed up for a while, Bob, but I'm all right now.
   B. I just didn't feel good, Bob. Old age coming on, I guess.
   C. I was just down in the dumps, Bob, but my doctor insisted that I go to the hospital. You know how they are.
   D. I'm glad to be back. What can I do for you, Bob?

KEY (CORRECT ANSWERS)

1. D
2. B
3. B
4. A
5. B

6. C
7. D
8. C
9. D
10. D

11. C
12. A
13. D
14. C
15. B

16. A
17. B
18. C
19. A
20. D

21. A
22. B
23. A
24. C
25. A

TEST 3

DIRECTIONS: Each question or incomplete statement is followed by several suggested answers or completions. Select the one that BEST answers the question or completes the statement. *PRINT THE LETTER OF THE CORRECT ANSWER IN THE SPACE AT THE RIGHT.*

Questions 1-7.

DIRECTIONS: Questions 1 through 7 are to be answered on the basis of the following information.

When Mark Levine, 5 1/2 years old, goes to school for the first time, he screams and seems terrified when he sees the drinking fountain near his classroom door. Mark's mother tells the school nurse that he has an intense fear of drinking fountains.

1. The understanding of Mark's fear of fountains that is MOST justifiable is that it   1.____

   A. is a symptom common in dyslexic children
   B. is not subject to his conscious control
   C. stems from his lack of understanding of plumbing
   D. results from having learned that his symptoms have a manipulative potential

2. Behavior therapy will be used in treating Mark's symptoms. His plan of care will include   2.____

   A. authoritative instruction
   B. increased cultural orientation
   C. direct interpretations
   D. systematic desensitization

3. Mark's behavior reflects his need to control anxiety by   3.____

   A. refusing to recognize the source of his anxiety
   B. making a conscious effort to avoid situations that cause anxiety
   C. substituting a neutral object as the target of his negative feelings
   D. acting in a manner opposite to his underlying need

4. Parents should be instructed that a child's mental health will BEST be promoted if the love he receives from his parents   4.____

   A. is related to the child's behavior
   B. is unconditional
   C. makes externally imposed discipline unnecessary
   D. is reinforced by unchanging physical demonstrations

5. Ms. Levine calls the community mental health clinic and tells the nurse that Mark has suddenly become terrified of getting into the family car, refuses to do so, and is in the yard screaming uncontrollably.   5.____
   What would it be BEST for the nurse to tell Ms. Levine to do FIRST?

   A. Hold Mark snugly and talk softly to him.
   B. Give Mark a warm bath and put him to bed.
   C. Bring Mark to the clinic as soon as possible.
   D. Remind Mark that he has never before been afraid of automobiles.

14

6. Mark is having play therapy.
   The choice of play therapy for children of Mark's age should PROBABLY be based upon their inability to

   A. overcome inhibitors about revealing family conflicts and behaviors
   B. differentiate between reality and fantasy
   C. recognize the difference between right and wrong
   D. adequately describe feelings and experience

7. On a rainy day, after Mark's play-therapy session, Ms. Levine hands Mark his overshoes and says, *Put them on. It's pouring outside.* Mark answers defiantly, *No, they're too hard to put on. I can't.* Then he sits down on a bench and pouts. Ms. Levine looks at the nurse in a perplexed way, saying nothing.
   Which of these responses by the nurse would probably be BEST?

   A. Say to Ms. Levine, *Maybe the overshoes are too small to Mark.*
   B. Sit on the bench with Mark and say calmly, *It's raining. You start pulling your overshoes on, and I'll help you with the hard part.*
   C. Hand Mark his overshoes and say to him in a matter-of-fact way, *If you will put the first one one, I'll put on the second one for you.*
   D. Say to Mark, firmly but kindly, *You are trying to test your mother's authority. This behavior will not be tolerated. Put your overshoes on right now.*

Questions 8-14.

DIRECTIONS: Questions 8 through 14 are to be answered on the basis of the following information.

Ms. Eileen Gray, 33 years old, is admitted to the psychiatric hospital with a diagnosis of obsessive-compulsive reaction. Her chief fear is that her excreta may harm others on the unit. As a result, she spends hours in the bathroom washing not only her hands, arms, vulva, and anal area, but also the walls, toilet, and toilet stall. In the process, she discards wet paper towels in every direction and leaves puddles of water everywhere.

8. Ms. Gray's symptoms are MOST clearly an example of

   A. sublimation of anxiety-producing fantasies and daydreams
   B. compensation for an imaginary object loss
   C. a symbolic expression of conflict and guilt feelings
   D. an infantile maneuver to avoid intimacy

9. On the unit, Ms. Gray carries out her elaborate washing routine several times a day. She says to the nurse, *I guess all this seems awfully silly to you.*
   It is MOST justifiable to say that she

   A. is asking the nurse to keep her from performing these unreasonable acts
   B. really believes her acts are completely rational, and she is testing the nurse
   C. is indicating an appreciation of the unreasonable-ness of her behavior
   D. is deliberately putting the nurse in a difficult position

10. The nurse should understand that the probable effect of permitting Ms. Gray to perform her washing routines will be to

    A. confirm a basic delusion
    B. help Ms. Gray to perceive how illogical her behavior is
    C. create distrust of the nurse, who ought to symbolize reality
    D. temporarily reduce Ms. Gray's anxiety

11. Ms. Gray is unable to get to the dining room in time for breakfast because of her washing rituals.
    During the early period of her hospitalization, it would be MOST appropriate to

    A. wake Ms. Gray early enough so that she can perform her rituals in time to get to breakfast
    B. firmly insist that Ms. Gray interrupt her rituals at breakfast time
    C. explain to Ms. Gray that her rituals are not helping her to get well
    D. give Ms. Gray a choice between completing her rituals or going to breakfast

12. During a nursing team conference, staff members voice frustration concerning Ms. Gray's constant questions such as *Shall I go to lunch or finish cleaning my room?* and *Should I go to O.T. or mend my coat?*
    In order to deal effectively with this behavior, team members should know that Ms. Gray's

    A. dependence upon staff is a symptom that needs to be interrupted by firm limit-setting
    B. inability to make decisions reflects her basic anxiety about failure
    C. indecisiveness is meant to test the staff's acceptance of her
    D. relentless need to seek attention represents a developmental arrest at the autistic (prototaxic) level

13. Ms. Gray is being treated by psychotherapy. The physician tells the nurse to expect her to be upset at times when she returns from her session with him and to let her be upset.
    By this directive, the physician MOST probably wants to

    A. put Ms. Gray under stress so that she will become more responsive to suggestions
    B. teach Ms. Gray to be satisfied with advice from only one person
    C. help Ms. Gray become aware of her feelings
    D. make Ms. Gray independent, which would not be possible if she were to develop alliances with members of the nursing staff

14. Ms. Gray is given her first pass to spend the night at home. As the time approaches for her to leave the hospital, she seems increasingly tense and says, *Maybe I shouldn't stay home all night. Maybe I should just stay for dinner and then come back here.* When the nurse responds nondirectively, Ms. Gray answers, *I'm just sort of anxious about things in general. It's nothing specific.*
    Which of these responses by the nurse would probably be BEST?

    A. Everyone is scared of his first overnight pass. You'll find that it will be easier than you expect.
    B. It's understandable that you are concerned about your first night at home. Would it help if you make the decision after you've been home for a while and see how things are going?

C. I know how you feel, but the staff think that you are well enough to stay home overnight. Won't you try to do so?
D. It's important for you to try to remain at home overnight. If you are able to do it, it will be a measure of your improvement.

Questions 15-25.

DIRECTIONS: Questions 15 through 25 are to be answered on the basis of the following information.

Ms. Kathy Collins, 47 years old, has been hospitalized several times over a period of years because of episodes of elation and depression. She lives with her mother and sister. She is well known to the nursing staff. While she is again being admitted, she is chainsmoking cigarettes, walking back and forth, and talking loudly and gaily about her romantic successes.

15. Which of these greetings by the nurse who is admitting Ms. Collins would probably be MOST appropriate?

    A. We're sorry you had to come back, Ms. Collins, but we are glad to see you.
    B. Good morning, Ms. Collins. Your doctor called to say you were coming. I will show you to your room.
    C. Hello, Ms. Collins. You're cheerful this morning.
    D. It's good to see you again, Ms. Collins. You don't seem to mind coming back to the hospital.

16. The nurse who will care for Ms. Collins each day should expect to make use of which of these interventions?

    A. Distracting and redirecting
    B. Orienting and reminding
    C. Explaining and praising
    D. Evoking anger and encouraging insight

17. Ms. Collins is an overactive patient with a mood disturbance rather than a thought disorder.
    Because of this type of illness, the nursing care plan should include measures that respond to the fact that she is

    A. disoriented
    B. easily stimulated by what is going on around her
    C. preoccupied with a single idea
    D. likely to be panicked by physical contact

18. Which of these nursing goals is likely to require the MOST attention while Ms. Collins is acutely ill?

    A. Orientation to time, place, and person
    B. Establishment of a sense of self-esteem
    C. Promotion of adequate rest
    D. Prevention of circulatory stasis

19. Ms. Collins and her roommate are in their room. While passing by, a registered nurse hears them arguing. Ms. Collins says, *You're a slob. How can anybody live in this mess!* The roommate answers, *What right do you have to say that?* and starts to cry. Which of these interventions by the nurse would be appropriate?

    A. Enter the room and say to Ms. Collins, *You have upset your roommate. She's crying.*
    B. Enter and say, *It sounds as if you are both upset.*
    C. Stand in the doorway and say, *It's part of your therapy to learn how to get along together.*
    D. Take the roommate aside and explain to her that Ms. Collins can be expected to be difficult for a few days.

20. Ms. Collins is not eating sufficient food. Which approach by the nurse would probably be BEST as a first step in trying to get her to eat more?

    A. Giving her foods that she can eat with her fingers while she is moving about
    B. Conveying to her tactfully the idea that she has to eat
    C. Serving her food to her on a tray and telling her firmly but kindly to eat
    D. Assuring her that she can have anything she wants to eat whenever she wants it

21. The physician orders lithium carbonate for Ms. Collins. To accompany the order for lithium carbonate, the physician is likely to specify that

    A. the patient should lie down for a half hour after each dose
    B. the medication should be evenly distributed throughout each 24-hour period
    C. a salt-free diet should be provided for the patient
    D. the drug level of the patient's blood should be monitored regularly

22. When their desires are frustrated, patients such as Ms. Collins are likely to

    A. maintain a superficial affability
    B. sulk and retire temporarily from the situation
    C. suddenly show hostility and aggression
    D. seek support from personnel

23. Group psychotherapy is ordered for Ms. Collins. The CHIEF purpose of this therapy is to help her to

    A. socialize easily with a group
    B. gain self-knowledge through the sharing of problems
    C. identify various types of emotional problems and ways in which people handle them
    D. become acquainted with types of problems that will be encountered after discharge

24. After several days, Ms. Collins' behavior changes, and she becomes depressed. One night the nurse finds Ms. Collins unconscious in bed with a strip of her sheet tied around her neck. She is cyanotic and her respirations are labored and stertorous. After loosening the constriction around Ms. Collins' neck and signaling for help, which of these actions by the nurse would demonstrate the BEST judgment?

    A. Remain with her.
    B. Place her in the proper position and start artificial respiration.

C. Give her a vigorous thump on the sternum.
D. Raise the foot of her bed.

25. Ms. Collins is gradually improving, and the team talks of plans for her discharge. On a visit to the unit, Ms. Collins' mother and sister tell the nurse that Ms. Collins doesn't seem much better, and they are very hesitant about having her return home because of the previous problems they've had with her. Which of these actions should INITIALLY be taken by the nurse?

    A. Suggest that the family find a place where Ms. Collins can live by herself after discharge.
    B. Elaborate on Ms. Collins' hospital regimen and the normality of her present behavior.
    C. Assure the relatives that Ms. Collins is better and refer them to the physician if they have further questions.
    D. Listen to Ms. Collins' relatives and suggest that they make an appointment with the family counselor.

25.____

KEY (CORRECT ANSWERS)

1.	B	11.	A
2.	D	12.	B
3.	C	13.	C
4.	B	14.	B
5.	A	15.	B
6.	D	16.	A
7.	B	17.	B
8.	C	18.	C
9.	C	19.	B
10.	D	20.	A

21.	D
22.	C
23.	B
24.	A
25.	D

EXAMINATION SECTION
TEST 1

DIRECTIONS: Each question or incomplete statement is followed by several suggested answers or completions. Select the one the BEST answers the question or completes the statement. *PRINT THE LETTER OF THE CORRECT ANSWER IN THE SPACE AT THE RIGHT.*

1. Which of the following offers the BEST description of the target of a crisis intervention?   1.____

   A. Displays of emotion
   B. Attitudes about loss
   C. Long-term consequences
   D. Specific, observable difficulties

2. Crisis intervention has become an important tool in assisting domestic violence victims because   2.____

   A. research indicates that it protects a person from future stress
   B. most individuals do not use their usual coping strategies when confronted with crises
   C. the outcome of a crisis has a great impact on a person's subsequent adjustment
   D. it reassures people that they could have coped with the stressor without help

3. A domestic violence professional is conducting an initial crisis interview with a client. During this first interview she begins to recognize a number of similarities between the woman's situation and one she, the professional, experienced a number of years ago, before she made the decision to leave her husband. The professional is careful to avoid a transference reaction in working with this client. Such reactions are LEAST likely to occur if the work with the client   3.____

   A. focuses on the here and now
   B. explores early life experiences
   C. is brief but intensive, involving several sessions a week
   D. analyzes intrapsychic processes

4. Typically, for a victim of domestic violence who is in crisis, coping mechanisms or responses that would be considered effective include   4.____

   A. the assumption that the beating was justified
   B. depression
   C. shock and anger
   D. an inability to decide what to do

5. According to Roberts' seven-stage crisis intervention model, which of the following procedures in a crisis intervention is typically performed LAST?   5.____

   A. Generating and exploring alternatives
   B. Developing and formulating an action plan
   C. Identifying major problems
   D. Planning and conducting a thorough assessment

6. During the initial assessment in a planned crisis intervention for a domestic violence victim, the professional finds that the victim cannot clearly identify the events that led her to seek help. The FIRST thing the professional should do is

   A. explain his/her own qualifications and expertise in dealing with such situations
   B. ask when the victim began to feel so upset
   C. identify the resources that are at the victim's disposal
   D. ask the victim who is responsible for these feelings of confusion

7. Each of the following is a guideline for a victim assistant's participation in crisis intervention procedures, EXCEPT

   A. expressing empathy by saying things such as "I understand"
   B. asking the victim to describe the event
   C. letting the victim talk for as long as he or she likes without interruption
   D. asking the victim to describe his or her reactions and responses

8. Once a victim of domestic violence has inappropriately internalized blame for the actions of the abuser and takes on the identify of victim, the main obstacle to the proper channeling of anger toward personal healing is usually

   A. violence toward others
   B. feelings of helplessness
   C. further abuse
   D. isolation

9. In working toward the accomplishment of ongoing goals in crisis intervention with a domestic violence victim, it is important to plan tasks that

   A. involve incremental changes that build on each other
   B. make few demands on the victim's outside resources or helpers
   C. are unlikely to prompt anxiety and hesitation
   D. demand large-scale and sweeping changes from the client

10. Effective crisis assessment skills and techniques include each of the following, EXCEPT

    A. an indirect approach that is not too emotionally upsetting to the victim
    B. the ability to empathize or appreciate another person's perspective
    C. an ability to appreciate the depth of another person's despair
    D. the willingness to address frightening experiences head-on

11. The culminating stage of personal crisis, described by many as "active crisis," is typically characterized by each of the following, EXCEPT

    A. an unbearable degree of tension and anxiety
    B. an unsolved problem
    C. a lack of internal and social support
    D. dissociative behavior

12. The first responsibility of a law enforcement officer who responds to a domestic violence incident in which the abuser has been accused of rape is to

    A. determine immediate medical needs
    B. arrange to transport the victim immediately to the hospital
    C. encourage the victim to shower and change clothes in order to feel better
    D. get the victim to sign an affidavit stating that he or she intends to cooperate with the investigation

13. During the assessment stage of a planned crisis intervention, a professional works with a client on identifying both *hazardous events* that have been experienced historically by the client and the *precipitating factor* that pushed the victim from a state of vulnerability into crisis. This process can help

    A. formulate questions about the victim's early emotional development and family life
    B. distinguish between chronic stress and an acute crisis state
    C. interpret the victim's emotional and cognitive reactions to hazardous events
    D. identify the existence of coping mechanisms

14. The crisis intervention techniques used by a professional should be derived according to the

    A. latest research findings in effective techniques
    B. roles of functions required of the client that are not being performed as a result of the crisis
    C. client's existing set of coping skills and mechanisms
    D. way the person in crisis is thinking, feeling, and acting

15. In most cases, the first symptom of rape-related post-traumatic stress disorder (RR-PTSD) is

    A. avoidance behavior
    B. feelings of reliving the traumatic experience
    C. memory impairment
    D. social withdrawal

16. Skill in decision counseling is essential to the processes of crisis assessment, planning, and intervening. In decision counseling, the professional facilitates crisis resolution by helping the victim decide each of the following, EXCEPT

    A. who should be involved in solving the problem
    B. what problem is to be solved
    C. in what ways his or her life will be altered after the problem is solved
    D. by what means (how) the problem can be solved

17. Core facilitative conditions of effective crisis intervention include each of the following, EXCEPT

    A. benevolent neutrality
    B. respectful warmth
    C. genuineness or authenticity
    D. empathy

18. A woman contacts the domestic violence worker at a battered women's shelter for advice about how to handle her boyfriend's abuse, which has been going on for about six months. The two have been experiencing financial difficulties that often result in arguments. The arguments sometimes escalate to the point of pushing and slapping. Entry-point workers who deal with victims of domestic violence often make use of a 5-point assessment scale that is part of a comprehensive mental health assessment. On this scale, the victim mentioned above would be assigned a rating of

    A. 2
    B. 3
    C. 4
    D. 5

19. Each of the following is a common physical symptom of post-traumatic stress disorder (PTSD), EXCEPT

    A. inability to sleep/fitful sleep
    B. difficulty concentrating
    C. severe headaches
    D. irritability

20. Which of the following is NOT an example of "primary prevention" in treating the crisis of domestic violence?

    A. Undergoing psychiatric inpatient treatment
    B. Leaving the household
    C. Devising a safety plan
    D. Identifying and using community resources

21. During a crisis intervention, it is generally considered important to FIRST

    A. help the client to gain an intellectual understanding of the crisis
    B. help the client to establish or re-establish a social support system
    C. explore coping mechanisms
    D. help the client bring into the open his or her private feelings

22. Once a crisis assessment has been conducted by both the client and the professional, the two of them sit down to compose an action plan. At the professional's suggestion, they decide to confirm the plan in a service contract. Which of the following conditions would NOT be implicit in the contract?

    A. The crisis counseling relationship is a partnership
    B. The person in crisis is capable of making concrete decisions about the direction her life will take
    C. The person in crisis is, by nature of her situation, the party who to whom most of the contract's rights and responsibilities will be assigned
    D. The person in crisis is essentially in charge of her own life

23. Which of the following does NOT take place during the initial stage of the crisis-reaction-repair cycle?

    A. guilt   B. shock
    C. anger   D. phobia

24. Significant and typical behavioral signs that a person is in crisis include each of the following, EXCEPT

    A. rigid, programmed gestures and speech
    B. inappropriate emotional responses, such as laughter, when recalling events
    C. a change in social behavior, such as withdrawal from friends
    D. an inability to perform normal vocational functions in the usual manner

25. Goals that are defined by the professional and the client during the first crisis intervention session must be
    I. challenging to both client and professional
    II. stated in positive, rather than negative terms
    III. appropriate for the knowledge and skills of the professional
    IV. defined in explicit and measurable terms

    A. I and II
    B. I, II and IV
    C. II, III and IV
    D. II and IV

KEY (CORRECT ANSWERS)

1. D	11. D
2. C	12. A
3. A	13. B
4. C	14. D
5. B	15. B
6. B	16. C
7. A	17. A
8. B	18. A
9. A	19. C
10. A	20. A

21. A
22. C
23. D
24. A
25. C

TEST 2

DIRECTIONS: Each question or incomplete statement is followed by several suggested answers or completions. Select the one the BEST answers the question or completes the statement. *PRINT THE LETTER OF THE CORRECT ANSWER IN THE SPACE AT THE RIGHT.*

1. In the crisis paradigm, the primary origins of the crisis of domestic violence are

   A. situational
   B. sociocultural
   C. transitional
   D. intrapersonal

   1.____

2. Which of the following is NOT typically a goal of crisis intervention?

   A. Addressing unresolved pre-crisis conflicts
   B. Preparation for managing future crises
   C. Regaining equilibrium
   D. Alleviation of stress

   2.____

3. The "downward spiral" toward emotional illness experienced by many assault victims usually begins with

   A. the misassignment of responsibility for the violence and abuse
   B. a turning away from potential sources of help
   C. a transition from acute to chronic anxiety
   D. the onset of vague suicidal thoughts

   3.____

4. The "Level I " assessment that begins the crisis intervention process focuses on the question of

   A. the potential threat to life
   B. how the person has responded to the situation or event
   C. identifying the hazardous event
   D. whether the person is in the acute or chronic phase of crisis

   4.____

5. What is the typical time-frame for crisis intervention?

   A. One to two weeks
   B. Six to eight weeks
   C. At least eight weeks
   D. Six months or more, depending on the nature of the crisis

   5.____

6. A domestic violence professional, after conducting a crisis assessment, refers a client to a crisis counseling group that is administered by a private subcontractor. In a follow-up session, the client tells the professional that she's enjoying the sessions and thinks the leader has been very helpful in solving some of her own problems. This week, she will be attending the eighteenth group meeting.
   Group crisis counseling that extends beyond ten sessions usually indicates one of the following, EXCEPT that the

   6.____

A. person in crisis has underlying, chronic mental health problems that should be dealt with in a traditional group therapy session
B. person in crisis may be substituting the group meetings for other, more regular social contacts
C. group is too large for the members to focus on the crises of individual members
D. counselor does not recognize the difference between crisis counseling and longer-term therapy

7. In an assessment interview with a woman who has just been hospitalized after being severely beaten by her husband, the professional asks the woman questions such as "How do you feel about what happened?" and "How do you usually handle it when your husband hurts you like this?" The answers to questions like these are useful for
   I. providing essential information about whether a person is in crisis
   II. linking the assessment process to intervention strategies by providing baseline data for action
   III. determining whether the victim's problem-solving skills and coping mechanisms are healthy or unhealthy
   IV. providing information about the meaning of stressful life events to the victim, and about her particular definition of the situation

   A. I only
   B. I and III
   C. II and IV
   D. I, II, III and IV

8. Which of the following is NOT a stage in the crisis-reaction-repair cycle?

   A. reinstitution
   B. reorganization
   C. recoil
   D. impact

9. A good crisis intervention plan
   I. is dynamic and renegotiable
   II. compels the client to achieve a different level of functionality
   III. is open-ended to allow for client singularities
   IV. is attitude-oriented

   A. I only
   B. I and II
   C. III and IV
   D. I, II, III and IV

10. In the context of crisis intervention, the most appropriate definition of "crisis" for the helping professional would be

    A. the suffering of a hazardous event
    B. alienation from a group that accepts one as a member
    C. the sudden loss or threat of loss of a thing considered essential and important
    D. a confusion or misinterpretation of self-identity

11. Each of the following are common psychological symptoms of post-traumatic stress disorder (PTSD), EXCEPT

    A. antisocial behavior
    B. decreased ability to feel emotions
    C. inability to remember parts of the traumatic event
    D. detachment from persons or activities which were formerly important to the victim

12. In crisis assessment, the identification of hazardous events or situations and the precipitating factor must be placed in a meaningful context. This is done by

    A. compiling all relevant facts about the situation
    B. determining whether the person's distress is great enough to be a risk to her life or the lives of others
    C. discovering the subjective reactions of the victim to stressful events
    D. probing the victim's past

13. During the "acute" phase following a rape or sexual assault, the two primary emotions felt by the victim are

    A. anger and sadness
    B. confusion and denial
    C. fear and self-blame
    D. sorrow and hopelessness

14. The task-centered model of crisis intervention is

    A. stylistic
    B. sharply focused
    C. confrontational
    D. open-ended

15. Using the family-centered approach to crisis assessment in a domestic violence situation can help the professional avoid

    A. further battering episodes
    B. under-identifying the number of family members who are in crisis
    C. transference reactions
    D. the apparent assignment of blame for the crisis

16. Which of the following is NOT considered to be a general factor involved in the function of crisis intervention?

    A. Establishing a long-term therapeutic relationship
    B. Focusing on coping strategies and problem-solving behavior
    C. Resolving immediate problems associated with crime victimization
    D. A high level of therapist activity marshaling all resources to facilitate client readjustment

17. Crisis intervention work with clients who are feeling especially vulnerable such as victims of domestic violence often lead to an unhealthy relationship known as the "victim-rescuer-persecutor" triangle. Professionals who work with such clients can avoid the evolution of this relationship by

    A. making use of power and control tactics
    B. being clear about necessary time limits and their rationale
    C. emphasizing sympathy over empathy
    D. conducting attitude-based assessments of the client's needs

18. The nature of the crisis intervention model virtually dictates that most interventions consist of an average of about _____ sessions or less.

    A. 2
    B. 6
    C. 12
    D. 25

19. During the initial assessment in a planned crisis intervention for a domestic violence victim, the professional finds that the victim cannot clearly identify the events that led her to feel so anxious and confused. The professional proceeds to ask the victim of simple, direct questions about the time and circumstances of the events that have upset the victim. This questioning strategy is likely to

    A. have a calming effect as the victim begins to piece together events and create some order out of her confusion
    B. cultivate, in the mind of the victim, the image of a caring professional who take the lead in solving problems
    C. cause further confusion as the victim adds new events and factors into her mental state
    D. create further anxiety as the victim is forced to relive the traumatic events

20. According to Roberts' seven-stage crisis intervention model, which of the following procedures in a crisis intervention is typically performed FIRST?

    A. Establishing rapport with the victim
    B. Identifying major problems
    C. Planning and conducting a thorough assessment
    D. Dealing with feelings and emotions

21. The primary goal of crisis intervention can best be described as

    A. protecting the victim from a situation in which he or she has become more likely to experience a traumatic event than other people
    B. helping the victim to identify and endure the long-term consequences of a traumatic event
    C. protecting a victim from self-harm following a traumatic event
    D. helping the victim to identify and cope with the sense of "disequilibrium" in the aftermath of a trauma

22. The "rape trauma syndrome" is considered to be

    A. a form of post-traumatic stress disorder
    B. a form of therapeutic intervention
    C. a short-term reaction
    D. triggered by previctimization events

23. A crisis worker must master the aspects of skillful communication with people who are very upset. These skills include
    I. asking simple questions that produce "yes" or "no" answers
    II. convey empathy, caring and sincerity
    III. offering as much reassurance as possible, even if it seems unrealistic at the time
    IV. asking the victim to identify why he or she thinks the event occurred

    A. I and II
    B. II only
    C. II and III
    D. I, II, III and IV

24. A woman is admitted to the hospital after her husband has raped her at knifepoint. The same woman has been hospitalized several other times as a result of his physical abuse. Entry-point workers who deal with victims of domestic violence often make use of a 5-point assessment scale that is part of a comprehensive mental health assessment. On this scale, the victim mentioned above would be assigned a rating of

    A. 2
    B. 3
    C. 4
    D. 5

25. Once a crisis assessment has been conducted by both the client and the professional, the two of them sit down to compose an action plan. At the professional's suggestion, they decide to confirm the plan in a service contract. Receiving help on such a contractual basis usually has the effect of
    I. confirming the professional's leadership role in helping the client through the problem-solving process
    II. documenting for insurance purposes the goals and outcomes of crisis care
    III. enhancing the self-mastery and social skills of the client
    IV. facilitating growth through a crisis experience

    A. I and III
    B. II only
    C. II, III and IV
    D. I, II, III and IV

KEY (CORRECT ANSWERS)

1.	B	11.	A
2.	A	12.	C
3.	A	13.	C
4.	A	14.	B
5.	B	15.	B
6.	C	16.	A
7.	D	17.	B
8.	A	18.	B
9.	A	19.	A
10.	C	20.	C

21. D
22. A
23. B
24. D
25. C

EXAMINATION SECTION
TEST 1

DIRECTIONS: Each question or incomplete statement is followed by several suggested answers or completions. Select the one that BEST answers the question or completes the statement. *PRINT THE LETTER OF THE CORRECT ANSWER IN THE SPACE AT THE RIGHT.*

1. A relationship in which a patient becomes dependent on the nurse   1.____

    A. is always unprofessional
    B. is inevitably "bad" for the patient
    C. may be necessary temporarily
    D. impedes learning

2. Anxiety is the CHIEF characteristic of the   2.____

    A. immature personality
    B. psychoneurotic disorder
    C. involutional psychotic reaction
    D. mentally retarded adolescent

3. The mode of psychological adjustment known as regression can BEST be described as   3.____

    A. refusing to think of unpleasant situations
    B. changing to a type of behavior which is characteristic of an earlier period in life
    C. reverting to actions characteristic of an historically early or primitive code of behavior
    D. hostility towards persons or objects that prove frustrating

4. The CHIEF danger in the employment of escape mechanisms as a form of adjustment is that they   4.____

    A. do more harm than good
    B. are socially undesirable
    C. make the experience expensive
    D. leave the basic problem unsolved

5. In essential hypertension, there is a(n)   5.____

    A. *increase* in systolic pressure and a *decrease* in diastolic pressure
    B. *decrease* in systolic pressure and an *increase* in diastolic pressure
    C. *increase* in *both* systolic and diastolic pressure
    D. *decrease* in *both* systolic and diastolic pressure

6. The *initial* paralysis in cerebral vascular accident, regardless of cause, is the type known as   6.____

    A. spastic   B. paraplegic   C. flaccid   D. rigid

7. Cerebral hemorrhage *most frequently* occurs in males in the age range from   7.____

    A. 20 to 30 years   B. 30 to 40 years
    C. 40 to 50 years   D. 50 years and over

8. Hereditary progressive muscular dystrophy is a disease characterized by progressive weakness and final atrophy of groups of muscles.
Of the following statements about muscular dystrophy, the one which is LEAST accurate is that

   A. there is no known cure for muscular dystrophy at present
   B. muscular dystrophy is a disease of the central nervous system
   C. early signs of muscular dystrophy are frequent falls, difficulty climbing stairs, development of lordosis, and a waddling gait
   D. therapeutic exercises may have some temporary value in the treatment of muscular dystrophy

9. The home care program is an extension of the hospital's service into the home on an extra-mural basis.
Of the following statements, the one that BEST explains the success of this program is that it

   A. *recognizes* the value to the patient and his family of the preservation of normal family life despite the limitations imposed by the patient's illness
   B. *makes* more hospital beds available for acute illnesses and emergency care
   C. reduces the cost of hospital care by reducing the number of inpatients
   D. *simplifies* hospital administration by reducing the number of chronically ill in hospitals

10. The MOST important of the following reasons for the rehabilitation of the seriously handicapped individual is that

    A. hospitalization of the handicapped is usually prolonged and costly to the community
    B. beds occupied by such patients reduce the number of hospital beds available for acutely ill patients
    C. care of chronically ill or handicapped patients is taxing and difficult for the family, the nurse, and the doctor
    D. it is important to the patient that he be as independent and useful as possible

11. There has been a notable increase in the discharge rate from mental institutions in the state during recent years. This change in statistics may be attributed CHIEFLY to

    A. increasing use of psychoanalysis and better trained personnel
    B. new drugs, changes in admission procedures, and the "open door" policy
    C. the increase in nursing homes for the elderly
    D. the use of psychotherapeutics and early diagnosis of mental illness

12. The PRINCIPAL and BASIC objective of mental hygiene is to

    A. modify attitudes as well as unhealthy behavior secondary to unhealthy attitudes
    B. care for the post-hospitalized psychiatric patient at home
    C. increase mental hygiene clinic services
    D. stimulate interest in improved education for doctors, nurses, and teachers

13. Separation of a child from his own home and placement in a foster home often arouses adverse reactions in the child. Of the following, the one which is MOST serious for the child is

    A. homesickness
    B. withdrawn behavior
    C. rebellion against authority
    D. dislike of new people

14. Behavior problems of the adolescent school child can BEST be explained by the fact that

    A. the adolescent suddenly becomes aware of the opposite sex at this time
    B. the demands made on adolescents by intolerant parents create rebellion against authority
    C. during childhood there is a general disregard of the child's need for independence by parents and other adults
    D. adolescence is a transition period between childhood and adulthood which usually creates feelings of insecurity in the adolescent

15. Of the following, the behavior which is LEAST indicative of serious emotional maladjustment in an adolescent boy is

    A. lying and cheating
    B. shyness and daydreaming
    C. gross overweight
    D. association with a teen-age gang

16. The one of the following diseases which is caused by a birth injury is

    A. cerebral palsy
    B. meningitis
    C. hydrocele
    D. congenital syphilis
    E. epilepsy

17. A delusion is a

    A. disharmony of mind and body
    B. fantastic image formed during sleep
    C. false judgment of objective things
    D. cessation of thought
    E. distorted perception or image

18. The one of the following which is the MOST common form of treatment employed by psychiatrists in treating patients with mental disorders is

    A. hypnotism
    B. hydrotherapy
    C. electroshock
    D. insulin shock
    E. psychotherapy

19. A masochistic person is one who

    A. is very melancholy
    B. has delusions of grandeur about himself
    C. derives pleasure from being cruelly treated
    D. believes in a fatalistic philosophy
    E. derives pleasure from hurting another

20. Surgery is *ESPECIALLY* difficult during the Oedipal period because of the

    A. father attachment
    B. mental age
    C. castration anxieties
    D. rejection complex
    E. separation from siblings

21. A psychometric test is one which attempts to measure

    A. social adjustment
    B. emotional maturity
    C. physical activity
    D. personality development
    E. Intellectual capacity

22. The one of the following conditions which falls into the classification of a psychosis rather than psychoneurosis is

    A. anxiety hysteria
    B. schizophrenia
    C. neurasthenia
    D. convesion hysteria
    E. compulsion neurosis

23. The one of the following which BEST describes psychosomatic medicine is:

    A. The understanding and treatment of both mind and body in illness
    B. The treatment of disease by psychiatric methods only
    C. The separation of mind and body in medical treatment
    D. The psychological testing of all individuals
    E. A system of socialized medical planning

24. The one of the following conditions for which shock treatment is *FREQUENTLY* used is

    A. alcoholism
    B. Parkinson's syndrome
    C. multiple sclerosis
    D. schizophrenia
    E. diabetes

25. The one of the following conditions which is *NOT* caused by the dysfunction of endocrine glands is

    A. myxedema
    B. duodenal ulcer
    C. cretinism
    D. Addison's disease
    E. none of the above

KEY (CORRECT ANSWERS)

1.	C	11.	B
2.	B	12.	A
3.	B	13.	B
4.	D	14.	D
5.	C	15.	D
6.	C	16.	A
7.	D	17.	C
8.	B	18.	E
9.	A	19.	C
10.	D	20.	C

21. E
22. B
23. A
24. D
25. B

TEST 2

DIRECTIONS: Each question or incomplete statement is followed by several suggested answers or completions. Select the one that BEST answers the question or completes the statement. *PRINT THE LETTER OF THE CORRECT ANSWER IN THE SPACE AT THE RIGHT.*

1. Euphoria is a state of

    A. depression   B. elation   C. ideation   D. frustration

2. An ailment found only in older people is

    A. manic depression   B. dementia praecox
    C. senile dementia   D. tabes dorsalis

3. The permissive policy employed in some mental hospitals is associated with a(n)

    A. increase in assaultive behavior
    B. open door policy
    C. decrease in the use of physical restraint
    D. increase in the use of physical restraint

4. A symptom of dementia praecox is

    A. extroversion   B. tic paralysis
    C. unpredictability   D. cerebral hemorrhage

5. Substituting an activity in which a person can succeed for one in which he may fail is

    A. sublimation   B. projection
    C. rationalization   D. compensation

6. Rationalization is the result of

    A. believing what one wants to believe
    B. reflective thinking
    C. scientific thinking
    D. basing conclusions on fact

7. Delusions of persecution are typical of

    A. epilepsy   B. regression
    C. schizophrenia   D. paranoia

8. A person with an IQ of 85 would be classified as

    A. defective   B. normal
    C. dull average   D. borderline

9. The term describing physical symptoms that do not arise *ENTIRELY* from physical causes is

    A. organic   B. psychoneurotic
    C. psychosomatic   D. psychopathological

10. The mechanism of attributing one's own ideas to others is termed

    A. projection
    B. substitution
    C. sublimation
    D. rationalization

11. A child's tendency to pattern after his parents is known as

    A. identification
    B. projection
    C. compensation
    D. substitution

12. Stuttering in children USUALLY originates from

    A. physical handicap
    B. mentally deficient parents
    C. emotional handicap
    D. imitation of other stutterers

13. Acute intoxication may PROPERLY be labeled a psychosis because it involves

    A. intellectual limitations
    B. emotional inadequacies
    C. bodily disease
    D. a severe loss of contact with reality

14. The outstanding change, of the following, in the aging process is that the aged are

    A. irritable
    B. no longer self-reliant
    C. senile
    D. easily influenced by stress

15. Re-adjusting the older person to be somewhat self-sufficient is known as

    A. stabilization
    B. regeneration
    C. rejuvenation
    D. rehabilitation

16. The spastic child usually

    A. is mentally retarded
    B. is potentially schizophrenic
    C. requires speech training
    D. has poor vision

17. Insomnia refers to

    A. unconsciousness
    B. sleeplessness
    C. sleep walking
    D. insensibility

18. A drug recently introduced in the treatment of mental illness is

    A. streptomycin
    B. paramino-salicylic acid
    C. reserpine
    D. cortisone

19. In general, the sleep requirement for an aged person as compared to the sleep requirement for a young adult is

    A. less   B. more   C. the same   D. slightly greater

20. The MOST IMPORTANT aspect of the rehabilitation of a person who has suffered a stroke is the

    A. patient's emotional reaction to self
    B. doctor's attitude toward the patient
    C. nurse's attitude toward the patient
    D. family reaction toward the patient

21. If a patient tells a nurse that he is contemplating committing suicide, the nurse should

   A. not pay any attention, since people who threaten suicide seldom follow through
   B. urge him to consult a psychiatrist, since potential suicides need psychiatric help immediately
   C. be sympathetic. Her sympathy will divert him from his intention
   D. realize that he is a neurotic with whom she will try to work

22. The BEST advice you can give parents disturbed by their five-year-old child's habit of nailbiting is to tell them to

   A. find out what some of the pressures on the child are and try to relieve them
   B. paint the child's fingers with the product "bitter aloes"
   C. point out to the child that this is a baby habit and not desirable in a school child
   D. punish the child by not allowing him to watch television or go to the movies

23. In certain periods of development, anti-social behavior in young children is considered normal. However, of the following situations, the one which merits referral to a mental hygiene clinic is where

   A. a two-year-old persists in hitting his four- year-old brother
   B. a three-year-old develops enuresis when a new baby is brought into the home
   C. a four-year-old runs away from home at every opportunity
   D. a six-year-old is not friendly, has no "pals" after six months in school, and participates in activities only when compelled to

24. Learning occurs

   A. when the child's responses are adequate
   B. when a solution to the situation is obvious
   C. when the adult solves the problems
   D. None of the above

25. The FIRST emotions to become differentiated may be described as

   A. anger and fear
   B. anger and distress
   C. fear and delight
   D. delight and distress

KEY (CORRECT ANSWERS)

1. B
2. C
3. B
4. C
5. D

6. A
7. D
8. C
9. C
10. A

11. A
12. C
13. D
14. D
15. D

16. C
17. B
18. C
19. A
20. A

21. B
22. A
23. D
24. A
25. D

EXAMINATION SECTION
TEST 1

DIRECTIONS: Each question or incomplete statement is followed by several suggested answers or completions. Select the one that BEST answers the question or completes the statement. *PRINT THE LETTER OF THE CORRECT ANSWER IN THE SPACE AT THE RIGHT.*

1. Marked improvement in a child's ability to draw a man over a brief period of time is MOST likely to be related to

    A. better social adjustment
    B. maturational effect
    C. the overcoming of a reading disability
    D. recovery from an illness

    1.____

2. Phenylketonuria, which is associated with intellectual disability, is a disorder of

    A. the reticuloendothelia system
    B. metabolism
    C. cerebral damage
    D. gyral defect

    2.____

3. A patient asserts, *I can't stand the agony I suffer when I go against my mother's wishes.* The therapist replies, *You really like to punish that momma inside of you for your dependency, don't you?*
This response can be viewed as an example of

    A. reassurance   B. interpretation
    C. support   D. reflection of feeling

    3.____

4. A shy young first grade boy becomes extremely attached to his teacher. He brings her presents, asks her to help him with his clothing a great deal, and wants to sit near her all the time.
He is MOST likely manifesting the mental mechanism of

    A. introjection   B. sublimation
    C. reaction-formation   D. transference

    4.____

5. The peculiarities of language behavior in the schizophrenic arise from his extreme need of a feeling of

    A. personal security   B. self-denial
    C. isolation   D. disarticulation

    5.____

6. The theory that psychical compensation for a feeling of physical or social inferiority is responsible for the development of a psychoneurosis is attributed to

    A. Adler   B. Horney   C. Freud   D. Sullivan

    6.____

7. Which of the following terms refers to the maintenance of stability in the physiological functioning of the organism?

    A. Functional autonomy
    B. Canalization
    C. Homeostasis
    D. Maturation

8. Extensive studies of the personality and behavior of intellectually gifted children generally reveal that they

    A. are physically better developed on the whole than average children
    B. are more likely to be emotionally disturbed than average children
    C. are more prone to divorce in later life than average children
    D. more often come from homes in which emotional disturbance is present

9. Expert opinion of professional workers with the physically handicapped indicates that a list of behavior characteristics would be headed generally by feelings of

    A. aggression   B. hostility   C. inferiority   D. courage

10. Children with pykno-epilepsy suffer from _____ convulsions.

    A. diencephalic
    B. visceral
    C. psychic equivalent
    D. no

11. Children with albinism and aniridia may read MOST comfortably with levels of illumination that, in relation to average levels of illumination, are

    A. upper   B. middle   C. lower   D. uneven

12. Phenylpyruvic amentia has been traced to which of the following?

    A. Nutritional deficiency in the prenatal environment
    B. A single recessive gene
    C. Pathological nidation
    D. Effects of radiation

13. Age of mother has been found to be MOST closely associated with the incidence of which of the following?

    A. Cerebral palsy
    B. Cerebral angiomatosis
    C. Down syndrome
    D. Hydrocephaly

14. The so-called visual area of the cerebral cortex is located in the _____ lobe.

    A. frontal
    B. parietal
    C. occipital
    D. temporal

15. Hypothyroidism is due to _____ in childhood.

    A. thyroid insufficiency
    B. pituitary insufficiency
    C. thyroid excess
    D. pituitary excess

16. The inability to express oneself in words in spite of an adequate understanding and imaginal representation is called

    A. agraphia   B. aphemia   C. agnosia   D. aphexia

17. Clara Thompson saw psychoanalysis as a method of therapy primarily designed to 17._____

    A. give the individual new insights into his past experiences
    B. help the individual master his difficulties in living
    C. have the individual re-enact his relationships with his parents
    D. strengthen the individual's ego defenses

18. According to Freud, the source of the large majority of the dreams recorded during analysis is 18._____

    A. a recent and psychologically significant event which is directly represented in the dream
    B. several recent and significant events which are combined by the dream into a single whole
    C. one or more recent and significant events which are represented in the dream-content by allusion to a contemporary but indifferent event
    D. a subjectively significant experience which is constantly represented in the dream by allusion to a recent but indifferent impression

19. When an individual permits unpleasant impulses or thoughts access to consciousness but does not permit their normal elaboration in associative connections and in affect, the psychoanalytic adjustment mechanism involved is 19._____

    A. rationalization   B. conversion
    C. isolation   D. introjection

20. In psychoanalytic thinking, repression can BEST be thought of as a(n) 20._____

    A. attempt in projection
    B. special type of introjection
    C. reflection of acceptance of Id impulses
    D. temporal form of regression

KEY (CORRECT ANSWERS)

1.	A	11.	C
2.	B	12.	B
3.	B	13.	C
4.	D	14.	C
5.	A	15.	A
6.	A	16.	B
7.	C	17.	B
8.	A	18.	D
9.	C	19.	C
10.	D	20.	D

TEST 2

DIRECTIONS: Each question or incomplete statement is followed by several suggested answers or completions. Select the one that BEST answers the question or completes the statement. *PRINT THE LETTER OF THE CORRECT ANSWER IN THE SPACE AT THE RIGHT.*

1. The behavior pattern considered to be deviate by clinicians is

   A. infractions of the moral code
   B. generosity
   C. recessive personality
   D. resistance to authority

2. A symptom of dementia praecox is

   A. tick paralysis
   B. negativism
   C. extroversion
   D. eremophobia

3. According to classic psychoanalytic thinking, the disorder MOST responsive to psychoanalytic therapy is

   A. compulsive neurosis
   B. hysteria
   C. narcissistic neurosis
   D. obsessive neurosis

4. For the therapist, the MOST common meaning of resistance is that it is a(n)

   A. index of lack of suitability for treatment
   B. defensive attempt on the part of the patient
   C. reflection of superior therapeutic promise
   D. relatively rare phenomenon in psychotherapy

5. In a normal distribution, the percentage of children whose IQ's fall between 90 and 110 is APPROXIMATELY

   A. 40   B. 50   C. 60   D. 70

6. The pioneer in mental diseases who was the first to make a distinction between emotional disorder and intellectual disability was

   A. Kraepelin   B. Seguin   C. Esquirol   D. Galton

7. In psychoanalytic thinking, the term superego generally embraces the

   A. necessary social prohibitions as well as the higher cultural strivings and ideals
   B. unconscious strivings of the person as well as the ego-ideal
   C. unconscious reproaches of the person as well as the id strivings
   D. unconscious ego and its defense mechanism as well as the ego-ideal

8. A major contribution of Fromm to psychoanalysis can be considered to be his

   A. attempt to formulate the dynamics of orality and the concept of original sin
   B. belief that man has innate social feeling and a drive for perfection
   C. effort to relate the psychological forces operating in man to the society within which he lives
   D. effort to integrate the concept of psychosexual development with Rankian principles

9. José, a ten-year-old, has a hyperthyroid condition. It is MOST likely that his behavior will be characterized by

   A. shyness, withdrawal, and reticence
   B. negativism, aggressiveness, and uncooperativeness
   C. placidity, passivity, and psychomotor delays
   D. restlessness, irritability, and excessive activity

10. The etiology of intellectual disability which is attributed to mechanical damage to the fetus would be classified as

    A. exogenous
    B. endogenous
    C. heterogenous
    D. none of the above

11. The majority of children of intellectually disabled parents will have IQ's that in relation to the IQ's of their parents are

    A. somewhat lower
    B. somewhat higher
    C. lower for boys and higher for girls
    D. lower for girls and higher for boys

12. Stuttering and stammering are MOST likely to develop between the ages of _____ years.

    A. 2 and 5
    B. 6 and 9
    C. 10 and 13
    D. 14 and 18

13. Most cases of stuttering are PRIMARILY the result of

    A. changed handedness
    B. hereditary factors
    C. physiological defects
    D. emotional problems

14. Anorexia is a condition which manifests itself in a loss of

    A. vision
    B. appetite
    C. motor control
    D. smell

15. Most differences in play activities and interests between boys and girls in the elementary school years can PROBABLY be attributed to

    A. inherent biological differences
    B. inherent emotional differences
    C. instinctual influences
    D. cultural influences

16. The rate and pattern of early motor development of children depend MAINLY upon

    A. experience
    B. acculturation
    C. maturation
    D. training

17. Of the following, the BEST index of the anatomical age of young children is

    A. brain weight
    B. ossification
    C. basal metabolism
    D. dentition

18. When children of very superior mental ability are compared in size and weight with children of the same age whose mental ability is average, the former children are found to be

   A. above average
   B. average
   C. below average
   D. either above or below average, depending on the age level

19. The average child speaks his first word at _____ months.

   A. 6   B. 9   C. 12   D. 15

20. In Pavlov's classical study of conditioning, the unconditioned stimulus was the

   A. food
   B. bell
   C. salivation
   D. electric shock

21. Contemporary reinforcement learning theory suggests that the MOST effective learning takes place when correct responses are _____ and incorrect responses _____.

   A. rewarded; ignored
   B. rewarded; punished
   C. ignored; punished
   D. none of the above

22. According to the literature, girls tend to develop physiologically and socially about

   A. the same as boys
   B. one to two years more slowly than boys
   C. one to two years more quickly than boys
   D. none of the above

23. The mother of a newborn infant is told by her physician that she will have to have corrective surgery performed within the next 2 years. It is expected that the operation in addition to her convalescence will keep her away from her baby approximately one month. The period during which the separation would be LEAST advisable from the standpoint of the child's emotional development is between the ages of _____ months.

   A. 1 and 6
   B. 8 and 16
   C. 16 and 20
   D. 20 and 24

24. Of the following, the term to which empathy is LEAST related is

   A. sublimation
   B. identification
   C. introjection
   D. projection

KEY (CORRECT ANSWERS)

1.	C	11.	B
2.	B	12.	A
3.	B	13.	D
4.	B	14.	B
5.	B	15.	D
6.	C	16.	C
7.	A	17.	B
8.	C	18.	A
9.	D	19.	C
10.	A	20.	A

21. A
22. C
23. B
24. A

EXAMINATION SECTION
TEST 1

DIRECTIONS: Each question or incomplete statement is followed by several suggested answers or completions. Select the one that BEST answers the question or completes the statement. *PRINT THE LETTER OF THE CORRECT ANSWER IN THE SPACE AT THE RIGHT.*

1. Epilepsy is MAINLY associated with   1.____

    A. brain injury B. migraine
    C. dysrhythmia D. aggressivity

2. A disturbance of language perception and expression is called   2.____

    A. aphasia   B. amnesia   C. amentia   D. alexia

3. Alcoholism is MOST commonly connected with   3.____

    A. dysrhythmia B. neurosis
    C. psychopathy D. overt homosexuality

4. The polygraph is MOST useful for diagnosing   4.____

    A. epilepsy B. aggressivity
    C. deception D. brain damage

5. The electroencephalogram is MOST useful for diagnosing   5.____

    A. brain tumor B. epilepsy
    C. brain injury D. mental deficiency

6. Shock therapy was recommended for   6.____

    A. paranoid schizophrenics B. depressed psychotics
    C. severe psychoneurotics D. psychopaths

7. Prefrontal lobotomy had been recommended for   7.____

    A. aggressive psychotics B. apathetic psychotics
    C. paranoid psychotics D. psychopaths

8. Most authorities believe that mental deficiency is _____ hereditary.   8.____

    A. never   B. always   C. sometimes   D. rarely

9. Recent experiments utilizing glutamic acid in an attempt to raise the intellectual level of retarded children have resulted in   9.____

    A. inconclusive findings
    B. a marked temporary rise in intellectual level
    C. a marked permanent rise in intellectual level
    D. a slight temporary decline in intellectual level

10. An individual's Rorschach protocol may be MOST profitably interpreted in the light of his   10.____

    A. behavior while being tested B. case history
    C. other test results D. presenting problems

51

11. If a child is mentally retarded, his academic potential can be explained MOST readily to his parent in terms of the status of other children

    A. in his class
    B. of similar CA
    C. of similar MA
    D. of similar IQ

12. It is MOST probable that a school-age child characterized, on the basis of psychological tests, as a mental defective might, in fact, be

    A. epileptic
    B. deaf
    C. mute
    D. schizophrenic

13. The classroom behavior MOST characteristic of the brain injured child includes

    A. distractibility, hyperactivity, and lack of inhibition
    B. listlessness, withdrawal, and compulsiveness
    C. aggressiveness, fearfulness, and egocentrism
    D. perseveration, fatigue, and apathy

14. A child's MOST rapid rate of mental growth generally occurs

    A. during the first few months of life
    B. between the ages of 3-6
    C. between the ages of 6-12
    D. during early adolescence

15. A psychopath may be distinguished by the fact that he commits antisocial acts

    A. consistently
    B. without customary reaction to guilt
    C. without awareness of what he is doing
    D. violently

16. Of the following techniques, the one which is considered to be characteristic of non-directive or client-centered therapy is

    A. encouraging transference
    B. reflection of feeling
    C. free association
    D. permissive questioning

17. Psychoanalytic writers consider the MOST important aspect of an analyst's training to be his

    A. training in psychoanalytic concepts
    B. training in medicine
    C. training in analysis
    D. general psychological training

18. In the transference situation, it is MOST probable that there will be _____ feeling(s) between analyst and patient.

    A. positive
    B. negative
    C. neutral
    D. positive and negative

19. The sequelae of encephalitis

    A. are now preventable in virtually every case of the disease
    B. may become evident long after an acute attack of the disease
    C. respond readily to treatment when detected
    D. are physical and emotional but rarely mental

20. The mental mechanism most strongly EMPHASIZED in psychoanalytic formulations of schizophrenia is

    A. repression
    B. conversion
    C. projection
    D. regression

21. Paranoia differs from the paranoid type of schizophrenia in

    A. the occurrence of delusions in one and not the other
    B. the fact that the paranoid patient does not act on the basis of his delusions
    C. the amount of *psychopathic tainting* in the family history
    D. that the delusions are more systematized

22. According to the Freudian psychoanalysts, the personality changes in general paresis are due to

    A. oedipus complex
    B. infantile sex urges
    C. sublimations
    D. changes in narcissism

23. A patient who touched his chin when asked to touch his nose would be MOST likely to be suffering from

    A. motor apraxia
    B. motor ataxia
    C. sensory apraxia
    D. agnosia

24. Shock treatment for schizophrenia, especially by the use of metrazol, was introduced at first because of the theory that

    A. shock arouses special physiological defense mechanisms by way of the *alarm reaction*
    B. shock stimulates the autonomic nervous sytem and thus facilitates homeostasis
    C. convulsions protect epileptics against developing schizophrenic symptoms
    D. shock as a form of punishment gratifies the patient's masochistic tendencies

25. From his survey of experimental evidence on the effect of infant care on later personality, Orlansky was led to the conclusion that such factors as breastfeeding and toilet-training

    A. are of no significance for later personality
    B. are significant determiners of personality
    C. are relevant to personality only insofar as they indicate the mother's attitude, which is the effective factor
    D. may help determine personality but constitutional and post-infantile factors should receive major emphasis

KEY (CORRECT ANSWERS)

1. C
2. A
3. B
4. C
5. B

6. B
7. A
8. C
9. A
10. B

11. C
12. D
13. A
14. A
15. B

16. B
17. C
18. D
19. B
20. D

21. D
22. D
23. A
24. C
25. D

TEST 2

DIRECTIONS: Each question or incomplete statement is followed by several suggested answers or completions. Select the one that BEST answers the question or completes the statement. *PRINT THE LETTER OF THE CORRECT ANSWER IN THE SPACE AT THE RIGHT.*

1. A part of the nervous system NOT known to have any connection with emotional behavior is referred to as the 1.____

   A. parasympathetic nervous system
   B. basal ganglia
   C. frontal lobes of cerebral cortex
   D. temporal lobes of cerebral cortex

2. A phobia is _____ anxiety. 2.____

   A. less specific than   B. more specific than
   C. synonymous with an D. less acute than

3. The division of the autonomic nervous system that coordinates bodily changes in fear and anger is 3.____

   A. sacral   B. sympathetic
   C. emergency   D. cranial

4. The effect of familiarity in the case of inter-racial attitudes is 4.____

   A. dependent upon the nature of the contact
   B. a tendency to breed contempt
   C. greater understanding and acceptance
   D. of little importance one way or the other

5. Negativism is MOST typical of children at the age of _____ year(s). 5.____

   A. one   B. three   C. six   D. nine

6. Children's groups about the age of two typically show 6.____

   A. much cooperation   B. sex segregation
   C. parallel activity D. none of the above

7. In which of the following functions does development depend MOST completely upon maturation? 7.____

   A. Roller skating   B. Swimming
   C. Singing   D. Walking

8. In the first months of an infant's life, the baby's reflex responses are 8.____

   A. almost the only reactions the baby shows
   B. virtually absent from behavior
   C. more accurate than later in life
   D. less conspicuous than generalized mass reactions

55

9. Play and reading interests of boys and girls will be found to be most DIFFERENT at the age of _____ years.

    A. three   B. six   C. twelve   D. eighteen

10. The unsociability often reported for very bright children is MOST likely to be due to

    A. their biological makeup
    B. their complete absorption in intellectual pursuits
    C. their lack of personal attractiveness
    D. the absence of suitable companions

11. If we measure a number of individuals upon a variety of complex mental functions, we will find that the different functions show _____ relationship.

    A. a negative
    B. no
    C. a fairly high degree of positive
    D. practically a perfect positive

12. Of the following general statements about deterioration in mental patients, which is the MOST questionable at present?

    A. More recently acquired forms of reaction are lost before those formed earlier in life.
    B. Generalization and abstraction in psychoses is qualitatively the same as that in the young child.
    C. Deterioration in many cases regarded as hopeless appears to be reversible.
    D. The responses of a deteriorated person show generally a definite patterning which tends to mask his defects.

13. Concerning the course of intellectual deterioration in the mental disorders, it is CORRECT to state that

    A. defect in the ability to generalize is more characteristic of schizophrenia than of other psychotic states
    B. concept formation deteriorates more slowly in schizophrenia than in senile psychosis
    C. decreased speed and persistence in mental activity are characteristic of epilepsy
    D. senile patients suffer more impairment in the recall of long past events than in recent memory

14. According to mental test comparisons of cooperative patients in the various disease groups, the group which shows the LEAST intellectual impairment is

    A. paranoid schizophrenia   B. psychopathic personality
    C. hebephrenic schizophrenia   D. hysteria

15. Schizophrenic speech is BEST characterized by

    A. loose, approximate use of words and reaction to superficial similarities among ideas and objects
    B. loose, approximate use of words and failure to make use of similarities or analogies

C. unusual amount of stammering and reaction to superficial similarities among ideas and objects
D. unusual amount of stammering and failure to make use of similarities or analogies

16. It is the central, distinguishing feature of the depressive phase of manic-depressive psychosis that the patient

   A. is keenly aware of lacking a motive for existence
   B. attaches his depression to some irrelevant or imaginary cause
   C. is excessively disturbed over some recent trouble
   D. is overactive, restless, and even agitated

17. In which of the following abilities do dull and gifted children tend to differ most markedly?

   A. Arithmetical computation
   B. Drawing
   C. Reading comprehension
   D. Spelling

18. The schizophrenic patient is said to exhibit loss of affect.
    This amounts to

   A. decreased attention to one's personal feeling tone
   B. lack of emotional reaction toward abstract ideas
   C. increased affectivity to ideas and decreased affectivity concerning persons and events
   D. increased affectiveness in environment but less to abstractions

19. Ability to establish a conditioned response in the eyelid has been found to be a point of differentiation between

   A. idiopathic epilepsy and hysterical seizures
   B. malingering and traumatic neurosis
   C. senile dementia and cerebral arteriosclerosis
   D. hysterical and organic blindness

20. The MAIN distinction between normal grief and reactive neurosis is in the

   A. feelings of inadequacy and unreality
   B. lack of basis in real occurrence
   C. duration and intensity of the emotional display
   D. intellectual retardation

21. Kretschmer's dysplastic type applies to those with

   A. compact, round, fleshy habitus
   B. strong, solid, muscular build
   C. slender bodies, long bones, little muscular strength
   D. conspicuous disharmony due to abnormal functioning of the endocrine glands

22. Which of the following is NOT characteristic of anxiety neurosis? 22.____

   A. Increase of irritable tension
   B. Vague somatic complaints
   C. Hypersensitivity to external stimuli
   D. Temporary muscular paralysis of the limbs

23. Involutional melancholia is usually characterized by a 23.____

   A. marked motor agitation   B. motor depression
   C. flight of ideas   D. loss of affect

24. From our knowledge about hallucinatory phenomena, it can be stated reliably that 24.____

   A. hallucinations occur in association with a dreamlike state
   B. hallucinations and imagery are similar processes differing only in intensity
   C. mescal-induced hallucinations are not similar to schizophrenic hallucinations
   D. organized hallucinations can be produced by direct stimulation of the brain surface

25. Which of the following is NOT a form of epilepsy? 25.____

   A. Grand mal   B. Pyknolepsy
   C. Jacksonian   D. Parkinsonian

KEY (CORRECT ANSWERS)

1. B   11. C
2. B   12. B
3. D   13. A
4. A   14. A
5. B   15. A

6. C   16. A
7. D   17. C
8. D   18. C
9. C   19. D
10. D   20. C

21. D
22. D
23. A
24. D
25. D

EXAMINATION SECTION
TEST 1

DIRECTIONS: Each question or incomplete statement is followed by several suggested answers or completions. Select the one that BEST answers the question or completes the statement. *PRINT THE LETTER OF THE CORRECT ANSWER IN THE SPACE AT THE RIGHT.*

1. A patient tells you that the other patients are plotting to kill him. This is MOST likely an example of

    A. a manic-depressive reaction
    B. a paranoid reaction
    C. excellent perceptual skills on the part of the patient
    D. a compulsive reaction

2. Which of the following statements is TRUE?

    A. Diagnoses are, by their very nature, always accurate.
    B. Phobic reactions are the most common reasons people are admitted to mental hospitals.
    C. People with neuroses are far less likely to be hospitalized than people with psychoses.
    D. Severely depressed patients are less of a suicide risk than any other patient group, except paranoid schizophrenics.

3. The LARGEST single diagnostic group of psychotic patients are

    A. neurotic depressive   B. schizophrenic
    C. obsessive-compulsive   D. paranoid reactive

4. The personality type that would BEST be characterized by the description that *he or she has no conscience* would be the

    A. drug addict   B. exhibitionist
    C. sociopath   D. manic-depressive

5. Of the following, the marked inability to organize one's thoughts is found MOST commonly and severely in

    A. schizophrenics
    B. amnesiacs
    C. those suffering from anxiety neuroses
    D. sociopaths

6. Someone who constantly feels tense, anxious, and worried but is unable to identify exactly why is MOST likely to be suffering from

    A. anxiety neurosis   B. schizophrenia
    C. dissociative reaction   D. a conversion reaction

7. A patient always insists upon twirling around six times before entering a new room, or she fears she will die. This is an example of

    A. paranoid reaction   B. obsessive-compulsive reaction
    C. dissociative reaction   D. anxiety neurosis

8. Of the following, those who suffer from neuroses would USUALLY complain of

   A. rejections, dissociation, and frequent inability to remember what day it is
   B. delusions, rejections, and feeling tired
   C. tiredness, fears, and hallucinations
   D. fears, physical complaints, and anxieties

9. The category that is caused by a disorder of the brain for which physical pathology can be demonstrated is

   A. neurotic depressive reaction
   B. schizophrenia
   C. functional psychoses
   D. organic psychoses

10. Of the following, which is NOT true?

    A. Someone who is suddenly unable to hear for psychological reasons would be considered to be suffering from a conversion reaction.
    B. If someone is in fugue, they have combined amnesia with flight.
    C. *Multiple personalities* is a dissociative reaction that affects primarily the elderly.
    D. General symptoms of schizophrenia include an ability to deal with reality, the presence of delusions or hallucinations, and inappropriate affect.

11. Which one of the following is TRUE?

    A. Calling an elderly person *gramps* or *granny* makes them feel more secure.
    B. It is important for an elderly person to maintain his or her independence whenever possible.
    C. When elderly patients start acting like children, they should be treated like children.
    D. It is important to encourage the elderly to hurry because they tend to move so slowly.

12. It has been found that older patients learn BEST when one does all but which one of the following?

    A. Allowing plenty of time for them to practice and learn
    B. Creating a relaxing environment for them
    C. Dealing with one thing at a time
    D. Assuming little knowledge on their part

13. Which of the following contains the main factors that should be considered before administering medications to elderly patients?

    A. How popular the medication is with the patient and the team leader's recommendations
    B. Any organic brain damage, liver dysfunction, and body weight
    C. Liver dysfunction, the patient's medical history, and decreased body weight
    D. Decreased body weight, impaired circulation, liver dysfunction, and increased sensitivity to medications

14. When communicating with the hearing impaired, it is BEST to do all of the following EXCEPT

    A. make sure the person can see your lips
    B. speak slowly and clearly
    C. use gestures
    D. shout

14.____

15. The three most common visual disorders in the elderly are cataracts, diabetic retinopathy, and glaucoma.
    Of the following statements about these, the one that is NOT true is that

    A. the symptoms for cataracts are a need for brighter light and a need to hold things very near the eyes
    B. diabetic retinopathy, if untreated, can cause blindness, so any vision or eye problems in diabetics should be promptly reported
    C. glaucoma develops slowly, so it is much easier to detect than cataracts or diabetic retinopathy
    D. some of the symptoms of glaucoma are loss of vision out of the corner of the eye, headaches, nausea, eye pain, tearing, blurred vision, and halos around objects of light

15.____

16. Which of the following is NOT true?

    A. Most of the elderly hospitalized for psychiatric problems suffer from senile brain atrophy or brain changes that occur due to arteriosclerosis.
    B. It is important to allow the elderly who wish to, the right to always live in the past.
    C. The majority of the elderly are competent, alert, and functioning well in their communities.
    D. Many elderly patients feel that they are no longer valued members of our society.

16.____

17. Of the following, which is NOT a good reason for helping the elderly patient stay active? Activity

    A. promotes good health by stimulating appetite and regulating bowel function
    B. prevents the complications of inactivity such as pneumonia, bed sores, and joint immobility
    C. can create an interest in taking more medication
    D. can increase blood circulation

17.____

18. Staff members must come to an understanding of their own feelings about the elderly because

    A. the staff may then be more helpful
    B. any negative feelings one has may be difficult to hide
    C. feelings of fear or aversion can be easily transmitted
    D. all of the above

18.____

19. An elderly patient will probably eat better if

   A. food servings are large
   B. the foods are chewy
   C. he or she is allowed to finish his/her meals at a leisurely pace
   D. cooked food is served cold

20. The MOST common accident to the elderly involves

   A. falls   B. burns   C. bruises   D. cuts

21. Which of the following is TRUE?

   A. Children should be considered and treated as miniature adults.
   B. Children are growing, developing human beings who will react to situations according to their level of development and the experiences to which they have been subjected.
   C. Children who are brought to a mental health center are usually calm and non-apprehensive on their first visit.
   D. The problems of adolescents are usually overestimated.

22. In working with adolescents, it would be BEST to

   A. neither bend over backwards to give in to demands, nor control them by rigid and punitive means
   B. dress the way most adolescents do
   C. staff those units with young people
   D. watch television with them regularly

23. Of the following, when working with children, it is MOST important to be

   A. consistent
   B. strict
   C. more concerned for their welfare than for the welfare of the other patients
   D. well-liked

24. Of the following, the element that is MOST lacking in relationships between adolescents and adults is

   A. respect   B. fear   C. trust   D. sensitivity

25. Of the following, the BEST reason for grouping children together would be

   A. they should be protected from the influences of all adult patients
   B. children tend to feel more comfortable with other children
   C. children are less likely to *act out* when they are with other children
   D. they would be unable to bother adult patients

26. All of the following statements are true EXCEPT:

    A. Accidents, reactions to drugs, fevers, and disease may each contribute to mental or emotional problems
    B. How effectively an individual reacts to and manages stress contributes to his or her mental health
    C. There is significant research that indicates that mental illness is caused primarily by genetic transmittal
    D. A person's upbringing, his or her relationships with family or friends, past experiences, and present living conditions may all contribute to the status of his or her mental health

27. All of the following are basic psychological needs which must be met for a person to have self-esteem EXCEPT

    A. acceptance and understanding
    B. trust, respect, and security
    C. a rewarding romantic relationship
    D. pleasant interactions with other people

28. All of the following statements are true EXCEPT:

    A. Most people become mentally ill because they are unable to cope with or adapt to the stresses and problems of life
    B. People with emotional problems can rarely be helped enough to live independently
    C. Most of the diseases and symptoms of the body which plague people have a large emotional component as their cause
    D. Environmental and familial factors are more important than genetic factors in mental illness

29. The following are all optimal aspects of family functioning EXCEPT

    A. communication is open and direct
    B. expression of emotion is more often positive than negative
    C. minor problems are ignored, knowing they will go away on their own
    D. there is a high degree of congruence or harmony between the family's values and the actual realities of the society

30. All of the following statements are true EXCEPT:

    A. People who are wealthy rarely become mentally ill
    B. Physical disease may influence emotional balance
    C. People who are mentally ill are often very sensitive to what is happening in their environment
    D. Most people doubt their own sanity at one time or another

31. All of the following statements are true EXCEPT:

    A. Hereditary factors are not the primary cause of mental illness
    B. A person may react to an extremely traumatic experience by becoming mentally ill
    C. Early recognition and treatment does not affect the course of mental illness
    D. Mental illness can develop suddenly

32. All of the following statements are true EXCEPT:

    A. Emotionally disturbed people are usually very sensitive to how other people feel towards them
    B. People do not inherit mental disorders, but may inherit a predisposition to certain types of mental problems
    C. There are many factors which can cause mental illness
    D. Mood swings are signs of mental illness

33. Which of the following statements is LEAST accurate?

    A. The difference between being mentally healthy and mentally ill often lies in the intensity and frequency of inappropriate behavior.
    B. The way a person views a situation determines his or her response to the situation.
    C. The mentally ill are permanently disabled.
    D. Different personal experiences cause a difference in what a person perceives as stressful, and how much stress a person can tolerate.

34. All of the following statements are true EXCEPT:

    A. Most experts in the field of mental health believe that the experiences which occur during the first twenty, or the first six, years of life are the most significant
    B. An unfortunate characteristic of children is that they tend to blame themselves for failures of their parents, and thus may develop feelings of inadequacy which may affect them all of their lives
    C. If neglect is severe enough, an infant or young child may withdraw from reality into a fantasy world which feels less threatening
    D. Human beings develop in the exact same pattern and almost at the same rate

35. Schizophrenia is

    A. genetically caused
    B. most often caused by the habitual use of drugs
    C. the result of a complex relationship between biological, psychological, and sociological factors
    D. most commonly caused by the inhalation of toxic gases

KEY (CORRECT ANSWERS)

1.	B	16.	B
2.	C	17.	C
3.	B	18.	D
4.	C	19.	C
5.	A	20.	A
6.	A	21.	B
7.	B	22.	A
8.	D	23.	A
9.	D	24.	C
10.	C	25.	B
11.	B	26.	C
12.	D	27.	C
13.	D	28.	B
14.	D	29.	C
15.	C	30.	A

31. C
32. D
33. C
34. D
35. C

TEST 2

DIRECTIONS: Each question or incomplete statement is followed by several suggested answers or completions. Select the one that BEST answers the question or completes the statement. *PRINT THE LETTER OF THE CORRECT ANSWER IN THE SPACE AT THE RIGHT.*

1. Tardive dyskenesia is a(n) 1.____

    A. antidepressant
    B. birth-related serious injury
    C. serious side effect of phenothiazine derivatives
    D. antiparkinsons drug

2. People taking psychotropic drugs are MOST likely to be sensitive to 2.____

    A. long exposures to sunlight
    B. darkness
    C. noise
    D. other patients

3. An antipsychotic drug that is a phenothiazine derivative would MOST likely be used for 3.____

    A. helping a patient lose weight
    B. calming a patient
    C. helping a patient sleep
    D. reducing the frequency of delusions in a patient

4. Of the following, an antidepressant such as Elavil would MOST likely be used for 4.____

    A. the immediate prevention of suicidal action in a newly admitted patient
    B. helping a patient lose weight
    C. elevating a patient's mood
    D. diuretic purposes

5. Which of the following statements is NOT true? 5.____

    A. Antianxiety tranquilizers such as sparine, librium, and vistaril are useful primarily with psychoneurotic and psychosomatic disorders.
    B. Minor or antianxiety tranquilizers tend to be less habit-forming than major or antipsychotic tranquilizers.
    C. Akinesia, pseudoparkinsonism, and tardive dyskenesia are serious side effects of antipsychotic drugs, or phenothiazine derivatives.
    D. Generally, those using tranquilizers like sparine or librium are in less danger of deadly drug overdoses than those using barbituates.

6. All of the following statements are false EXCEPT: 6.____

    A. Antipsychotic drugs promote increased sexual interest
    B. Patients no longer need to take their medication when they feel better
    C. Phenothiazines are psychotropic drugs
    D. One of the main difficulties with antipsychotic drugs is that they tend to be habit-forming

7. Yellowing of the skin or eyes, sensitivity to light and pseudoparkinsonism may occur in patients receiving 7.____

   A. mellaril or thorazine
   B. librium or tranxene
   C. valium or vistaril
   D. antiparkinson drugs

8. Which of the following is NOT true of extrapyramidal symptoms (EPS)? They 8.____

   A. may appear after many weeks of use of phenothiazines
   B. can safely be controlled without medical assistance
   C. may appear after the patient has been taking the drug for only a few days
   D. may include pseudoparkinsonism

9. The time required to reach an effective blood level for an antidepressant medication would MOST likely be three 9.____

   A. days   B. hours   C. weeks   D. months

10. An example of a psychotropic drug would be 10.____

    A. seconal   B. aspirin   C. librium   D. perichloz

11. In evaluating a patient you are meeting for the first time, it would be best NOT to 11.____

    A. be as objective as possible
    B. question one's own motives and reactions when processing data during and after the meeting
    C. be extremely goal-oriented
    D. not allow any praise or criticism directed at you by the patient to influence your assessment

12. All of the following statements are true EXCEPT: 12.____

    A. People communicate non-verbally via their behavior and their body posture
    B. Non-verbal clues may be a better indication of a patient's true feelings than what the patient actually says
    C. A patient who is highly anxious is easier to evaluate than a patient who is relatively calm
    D. People should be judged objectively

13. When asking a patient a question, one should do all of the following EXCEPT 13.____

    A. phrase questions in order to receive a yes or no response
    B. ask only relevant questions
    C. listen carefully to the response before asking the next question
    D. phrase questions clearly

14. The MAIN purpose for extensive record keeping is to 14.____

    A. provide an accurate description of the patient's diagnosis
    B. provide a subjective report of the patient's behavior
    C. provide an objective report of the patient's behavior
    D. give mental health personnel something to do

15. When talking to a patient for the first time, one must realize that

    A. hostile behavior indicates an extremely severe disorder in the patient
    B. a patient's physical appearance will indicate how successful you will be in communicating with the patient
    C. the patient is extremely nervous
    D. you are both strangers to each other

16. Of the following, which statement is NOT true?

    A. The rapid assessment of a patient is not necessarily accomplished by asking a series of routine questions.
    B. There is value, in assessing a patient, in creating a conversational bridge which has *here and now* relevance.
    C. One can assess a patient's state by his or her reaction to a warm greeting given to him or her.
    D. There is some value in routinely asking certain questions, when needed, in order to check a patient's orientation and memory.

17. All of the following could be signs that someone is moving towards mental illness EXCEPT

    A. exhibiting a degree of prolonged, constant anxiety, apprehension, or fear which is out of proportion with reality
    B. severe appetite disturbances
    C. occasional depression
    D. abrupt changes in a person's behavior

18. The first few minutes of interaction with a patient can reveal all but

    A. a patient's contact with reality
    B. whether you are comfortable with a patient
    C. a patient's mood
    D. a patient's chances for recovery

19. Which of the following statements is TRUE?

    A. The tentative diagnosis made when a patient is first admitted is the most accurate diagnosis.
    B. One should always try and keep in mind the state the patient was in when first admitted.
    C. A diagnosis is actually an ongoing process.
    D. When assessing patients' behavior, it is best to be suspicious of what may look like progress.

20. All of the following are examples of defense mechanisms EXCEPT

    A. projection   B. complimenting someone
    C. displacement   D. regression

21. A treatment plan is likely to be MOST effective if the

    A. patient's suggestions are always incorporated
    B. patient is voluntarily and wholeheartedly participating in the treatment plan designed for him or her

C. patient has daily contact with his or her family
D. patient respects the team leader

22. All of the following are true EXCEPT:

    A. Patients do not become well simply by people doing something for them
    B. A patient's well-being is enhanced when one or more team members can forge a *therapeutic alliance* with that patient
    C. The most important purpose of the treatment team is to administer the proper medications to patients
    D. It is important that a patient be seen as an individual, and not just as a *case* or a *number*

23. Of the following, a member of the treatment team can BEST assist a patient by

    A. commanding respect from other team members
    B. carefully observing the behavior of patients
    C. avoiding spending too much time with patients
    D. becoming friends with a patient

24. Of the following, which is LEAST important when considering a treatment plan?

    A. Involving the patient
    B. Setting reasonable goals
    C. Being as specific as possible in setting completion dates for goals, and sticking to them
    D. Detailing the methods to be followed, and the work assignments

25. All of the following are true EXCEPT:

    A. A treatment team should help patients understand that they can improve their condition if they will cooperate with the treatment plan
    B. Patients should be encouraged to participate in the programs designed for them
    C. Patients should be encouraged to revise their treatment plans
    D. One's approach should be tailored for each individual, whenever possible

26. All of the following could be considered appropriate goals for patients to work towards, EXCEPT to

    A. expand one's capacity to find or create acceptable options
    B. learn to be less dependent
    C. give up feeling persecuted
    D. learn how to get what one needs, at any cost

27. In working in treatment teams, it is MOST important for team members to

    A. communicate effectively with each other
    B. enjoy working with each other
    C. keep morale high
    D. attend meetings on time

28. One of the purposes of the treatment team is to

    A. decrease the amount of work
    B. coordinate and integrate services to patients
    C. provide training
    D. provide patients with basic counseling skills they can use

29. When working with someone exhibiting a manic-depressive psychosis, depressed type, it is BEST to

    A. concern yourself primarily with his or her eating habits
    B. focus primarily on their sleeping habits
    C. take every statement he or she may make about suicide seriously
    D. allow them to watch a great deal of television

30. In working with a paranoid patient, all of the following are true EXCEPT:
    It

    A. is important to listen with respect
    B. is helpful to establish a trusting relationship
    C. is good to try and talk the patient out of his or her fears
    D. would not be a good practice to agree with their statements, if they are not true

31. It is important, when dealing with verbally abusive patients, to keep in mind all of the following EXCEPT:

    A. Patients usually become abusive because of frustrating circumstances beyond their control
    B. In most cases, the patients do not mean anything personal by their abusive remarks; they are displacing anger
    C. It is important for staff members to remain calm and controlled when patients have emotional outbursts
    D. It is a good idea to allow an angry patient to draw you into an argument, as this will eventually help calm him or her down

32. When dealing with a patient who insists upon doing a number of rituals before brushing his teeth, it would be BEST to

    A. attempt to tease him out of his behavior
    B. not be critical of the ritualistic behavior
    C. perform the same rituals so that he feels more secure
    D. insist that he eliminate one step of the ritual each week

33. A patient tells you that he is balancing an automobile on the top of his head, and asks you what you think of that.
    An APPROPRIATE response for you to make would be:

    A. to ask him to take you for a ride
    B. *Stop saying ridiculous things*
    C. *I know you believe you are balancing a car on your head but I don't see it, therefore I have to assume that you're not*
    D. *Is it an invisible car*

34. A new patient, who is very paranoid, refuses to take off his clothes before getting into bed.
    Which would be MOST helpful?

    A. Getting another staff member to assist in removing his clothes
    B. Leaving the room until he comes to his senses
    C. Trying to find out why the patient does not want to undress
    D. Allowing the patient to stay up all night

35. In handling depressed patients, it is BEST to

    A. encourage them to participate in activities
    B. remind them often that things will be better tomorrow
    C. remember that depressed patients have few feelings of guilt
    D. let them know that you know just how they are feeling

36. A patient tells you that she is very depressed over the recent death of her brother. Which of the following would be the MOST appropriate response?

    A. *Everybody gets depressed when they lose someone they love.*
    B. *It could have been worse; at least he was ill only a short time.*
    C. *I know just how you feel.*
    D. *This must be very difficult for you.*

37. A patient who recently suffered a stroke refuses to let you help her bathe.
    This is probably because

    A. it is hard for her to accept that she can no longer do things for herself that she could do before the stroke
    B. she does not like you
    C. she is extremely independent and should be encouraged to be less so
    D. you need to review your methods for bathing patients

38. All of the following would be appropriate in working with a patient who is hallucinating EXCEPT

    A. carefully watch what you are non-verbally communicating
    B. ask concrete, reality-oriented questions
    C. provide a calm, structured environment
    D. agree with the patient, if asked, that you are experiencing the same state he or she is

39. In dealing with overactive patients, it is BEST to

    A. not give most of your attention to these patients, leaving the quieter patients to look after themselves
    B. keep in mind that overactive patients are always more interesting than other patients
    C. remember that overactive patients need more care than other patients
    D. forcibly restrain them whenever possible

40. A patient with mild organic brain damage is very withdrawn and negativistic. The BEST approach, of the following, would be

    A. *I need a partner to play cards with me*
    B. *Your family is very disappointed in you when you act like this*
    C. *Your doctor said you should participate in all activities here, so you'd better do that*
    D. *Would you like to go to your room so you can be alone?*

40.____

KEY (CORRECT ANSWERS)

1.	C	11.	C	21.	B	31.	D
2.	A	12.	C	22.	C	32.	B
3.	D	13.	A	23.	B	33.	C
4.	C	14.	C	24.	C	34.	C
5.	B	15.	D	25.	C	35.	A
6.	C	16.	C	26.	D	36.	D
7.	A	17.	C	27.	A	37.	A
8.	B	18.	D	28.	B	38.	D
9.	C	19.	C	29.	C	39.	A
10.	C	20.	B	30.	C	40.	A

EXAMINATION SECTION
TEST 1

DIRECTIONS: Each question or incomplete statement is followed by several suggested answers or completions. Select the one that BEST answers the question or completes the statement. *PRINT THE LETTER OF THE CORRECT ANSWER IN THE SPACE AT THE RIGHT.*

1. Clinical observations and research on motor functioning of the intellectually disabled indicate

    A. there is a marked discrepancy in motor functioning between tasks requiring precise and those requiring complex movements
    B. there is a high degree of correspondence between general mental ability and motor performance
    C. there is no difference in the motor performance of moderately disabled and mildly disabled individuals
    D. degree of stimulation has no effect on motor performance

2. The incidence of the diagnosis of intellectual disability in males as compared with that of females is

    A. considerably higher
    B. considerably lower
    C. slightly lower
    D. about the same

3. In terms of their behavior and the causes of their disability, intellectually disabled children would be classified as a _____ group.

    A. very homogeneous
    B. moderately homogeneous
    C. very heterogeneous
    D. moderately heterogeneous

4. In terms of socioeconomic status, MOST disabled children come from families that in socioeconomic status

    A. are rated low
    B. range from middle class to high
    C. are middle class
    D. range the spectrum

5. While phenylketonuria accounts for a small fraction of intellectual disabilities, it is one of the few forms that can be

    A. identified as a causative agent in the first three months of pregnancy
    B. vitiated by early psychiatric treatment
    C. alleviated through strict adherence to a high phenyla-lanine diet
    D. prevented by specific medical intervention

6. A child who has been diagnosed as having cerebral aphasia shows _____ speech.

    A. lack of   B. perseverative   C. echolalic   D. repetitive

7. Follow-up studies indicate that the intellectually disabled tend to

    A. remain on their initial job because they are fearful of change
    B. change jobs frequently in their early post-school years
    C. move up the ladder of success as do non-disabled, but at a slower pace
    D. stabilize in one job or one area of work in their early post-school years

8. The PRIMARY objective of special education for the preponderance of the intellectually disabled is

   A. contribution to the community
   B. participation in family life
   C. adjustment to the neighborhood environment
   D. adjustment in a sheltered work situation

9. Disability resulting from organic impairment or birth injury has been classified as

   A. endogenous
   B. familial
   C. primary amentia
   D. exogenous

10. Resources in the community for treating the emotional problems of intellectually disabled children are

    A. more difficult to obtain than for non-disabled children
    B. under-utilized because of parental resistance to accepting disabilities
    C. under-utilized because the disabilities tend to mask emotional difficulties
    D. not effective with most types of disabled children

11. The disabled child who refuses to attend school and cries, throws up, and clings to the parent when it comes time to leave each morning is MOST probably showing symptoms of

    A. overdependence
    B. school phobia
    C. psychopathic behavior
    D. improper nutrition

12. One of the MOST promising developments in institutional care for the intellectually disabled was the

    A. addition of attendants to the inter-disciplinary staffs of installations
    B. organization of a well-rounded recreation program
    C. inclusion of psychotherapy in the institutional program
    D. establishment of a self-government program

13. The Arc is a(n)

    A. youth group for the disabled, similar in design to the 4-H Clubs
    B. group of non-professionals associated with the American Association on Mental Deficiency
    C. service and support organization for disabled individuals and their families
    D. association of teachers of the disabled, organized by the National Education Association

14. In MOST instances, parental inability to accept disabilities in their child as a fact can be attributed primarily to their

    A. feelings of guilt
    B. fear of being viewed as subnormal themselves
    C. lack of knowledge of children's development
    D. being too close to the child to see him objectively

15. Which one of the following descriptions MOST accurately characterizes the degree to   15.____
    which the intellectually disabled will be able to function in social-vocational areas when
    they reach adulthood?

    A. Little more than self-care
    B. Partial self-support in a supervised environment, such as a sheltered workshop
    C. Employment, when given assistance from medical personnel in correcting physical
       or emotional deficiencies
    D. Employment in the community with the aid of appropriate school and community
       agencies when necessary

16. The process whereby an individual acquires his moral, social, and emotional attitudes   16.____
    from the people with whom he comes in frequent contact is called

    A. projection   B. introjection
    C. transfer of learning   D. transference

17. A resident of working age, who has a permanent disability that is an employment   17.____
    handicap, is eligible for vocational rehabilitation if he

    A. is unemployable
    B. requires custodial care for an extended period of time
    C. is employable in a sheltered workshop only
    D. can become employable within a reasonable length of time

18. Of those listed below, the MOST likely jobs for the intellectually disabled are: 18.____

    A. Messenger, hospital tray worker
    B. Foot press operator, practical nurse
    C. Shoeshine man, barber
    D. Plumber's helper, elevator operator

19. Of the following, which one is the MOST common etiological factor in clinical cases of   19.____
    intellectual disability?

    A. Phenylketonuria   B. Down syndrome
    C. Organic brain damage   D. Environmental deprivation

20. Which of the following types of recreational activity are MOST appropriate for the   20.____
    intellectually disabled?

    A. Basketball, swimming   B. Dancing, bowling
    C. Football, boxing   D. Stickball, roller skating

KEY (CORRECT ANSWERS)

1.	B	11.	B
2.	A	12.	D
3.	C	13.	C
4.	D	14.	A
5.	D	15.	D
6.	A	16.	B
7.	B	17.	D
8.	A	18.	A
9.	D	19.	C
10.	A	20.	B

TEST 2

DIRECTIONS: Each question or incomplete statement is followed by several suggested answers or completions. Select the one that BEST answers the question or completes the statement. *PRINT THE LETTER OF THE CORRECT ANSWER IN THE SPACE AT THE RIGHT.*

1. The instructional program for the intellectually disabled stresses

    A. association
    B. configuration
    C. perseveration
    D. habit formation

2. Of the following, the MAJOR goal of the education of disabled children is to enable them to

    A. become skilled workers in selected jobs
    B. develop a better understanding of their problems and make a better adjustment to them
    C. become completely socially adequate in their communities
    D. develop qualities of leadership in limited areas

3. The MAJOR way in which the development of the disabled child resembles that of the normal child in the early years of life is in the attainment of

    A. locomotion skills
    B. manual dexterity
    C. language skills
    D. physical size

4. The terminology used in characterizing the disabled has changed over the years. Which one of the following CORRECTLY gives the order in which past terms have appeared?

    A. Mentally deficient, mentally handicapped, feebleminded
    B. Mentally deficient, feebleminded, mentally retarded
    C. Feebleminded, mentally deficient, mentally retarded
    D. Mentally retarded, feebleminded, mentally deficient

5. As the severely disabled child approaches adolescence and adulthood, there is a tendency for the IQ to

    A. decline
    B. remain static
    C. show slight but positive increases
    D. show significant increases

6. When used with reference to intellectually disabled children, the term *adaptive behavior* refers to the child's

    A. ability to shift readily from one learning situation to another
    B. prognosis for anti-social behavior
    C. effectiveness in coping with the social demands of the environment
    D. functioning level as determined by a projective testing technique

7. In presenting areas of interest for the disabled adolescent:
    I. Budgeting
    II. Study of Job Areas
    III. The Worker as a Citizen and Social Being
    IV. Choosing, Getting, and Holding a Job

    The MOST appropriate sequence is

    A. II, IV, I, III
    B. IV, III, II, I
    C. I, II, III, IV
    D. IV, I, III, II

77

8. Studies comparing the forgetting of completed and incompleted tasks tend to show that

   A. completed tasks tend to be forgotten more rapidly than incompleted ones
   B. incompleted tasks tend to be forgotten more rapidly than completed ones
   C. there is no difference in retention of the two types of tasks
   D. the inconclusive results that have been obtained make it impossible to generalize

9. Of the following, which is generally MOST conducive to the mastery of a skill?

   A. The practice of the skill in a daily routine
   B. Emphasis on speed rather than accuracy in early practice
   C. Overlearning
   D. Lack of emotion and pressure during practice

10. Degree of maturity, amount of previous experience, and motivation are all factors affecting the degree of _____ shown by a learner.

    A. intelligent activity   B. transfer of skills
    C. readiness   D. retention

11. Of the following, which one is of relatively minor effectiveness in determining the amount of transfer of learning from one subject to another? The

    A. degree of relationship between the two subjects involved
    B. methods used by the teacher to establish a relationship between the subjects involved
    C. amount of study time put in by the learner on the material
    D. ability of the learner to make generalizations

12. Where there are no adequate public facilities for the instruction of an intellectually disabled child who can reasonably be expected to profit from such instruction, the parent

    A. may keep the child at home until a facility becomes available
    B. may educate the child privately, deducting the costs from state and federal taxes as legitimate medical expenses
    C. may register the child in a class conducted by a parents' organization in the state, with the state paying tuition charges
    D. can apply for state aid under an appropriate section of the Education Law

13. Learning and maturation differ from one another as forms of behavior development in that the latter

    A. depends on special training during a critical period
    B. is continuous, while the former is not
    C. must be externally prompted
    D. appears spontaneously

14. The long retention of skills such as swimming is generally explained by reference to the

    A. law of multiple response
    B. law of effect
    C. effect of overlearning
    D. process of redisintegration

15. Which one of the following psychologists identified the five stages (sensorimotor operations, preconceptual thought, intuitive thought, concrete operations, and formal operations) in intellectual development?

    A. Edward L. Thorndike
    B. Frances L. Ilg
    C. Jean Piaget
    D. Arnold Gesell

16. A practical application of the *stimulus-response* theory of learning is BEST exemplified in the classroom by the use of

    A. audio-visual aids
    B. experience charts
    C. developmental reading techniques
    D. teaching machines

17. Of the following, the use of the *conditioned-response* method of learning has been found MOST successful in dealing with

    A. enuresis
    B. epileptic seizures
    C. attitudes
    D. reading disabilities

18. The type of forgetting in which people tend to forget the names of persons they do not like is generally termed

    A. negative retention
    B. repression
    C. proactive inhibition
    D. retroactive inhibition

19. Experimental evidence suggests that the MOST effective learning and retention of material such as poetry takes place when the material is memorized

    A. as a whole unit
    B. word by word
    C. line by line
    D. stanza by stanza

20. The MOST recent theories of the causation of reading disabilities stress as a major factor

    A. perceptual dysfunctions and lags
    B. lack of cultural stimulation
    C. minimal brain damage
    D. lack of parental interest and aspiration

KEY (CORRECT ANSWERS)

1. D
2. B
3. D
4. C
5. A

6. C
7. A
8. A
9. C
10. C

11. C
12. D
13. D
14. C
15. C

16. D
17. A
18. B
19. A
20. A

EXAMINATION SECTION
TEST 1

DIRECTIONS: Each question or incomplete statement is followed by several suggested answers or completions. Select the one that BEST answers the question or completes the statement. *PRINT THE LETTER OF THE CORRECT ANSWER IN THE SPACE AT THE RIGHT.*

1. An effective method to correct mirror writing by the intellectually disabled is to
    A. have him write looking through a mirror
    B. have him change from use of left hand to the right hand
    C. re-emphasize the correct posture and position for writing
    D. have him copy models showing the starting point of writing

    1.____

2. Dr. Robert Guthrie developed a blood test to be administered to infants to detect the presence of
    A. syphilis
    B. hypothyroidism
    C. hydrocephalus
    D. phenylketonuria

    2.____

3. Which of the following defines intellectual disability as a disability characterized by significant limitations both in intellectual functioning and in adaptive behavior, originating before age 18 and covering a range of everyday social and practical skills?
    A. American Association on Intellectual and Developmental Disabilities
    B. E.A. Doll
    C. Council for Exceptional Children
    D. Clemens Benda

    3.____

4. Early studies on the nature of intelligence revealed that the BEST predictors of intelligence for school-age children were _____ tasks.
    A. simple sensori-motor
    B. complex sensori-motor
    C. speed of reaction to timed
    D. complex verbal

    4.____

5. Which of the following conditions automatically warrants the exclusion of intellectually disabled children from school attendance?
    A. Lack of toilet training
    B. Petit-mal epilepsy
    C. Aphasia
    D. Anxiety

    5.____

6. Which one of the following state agencies is assigned the responsibility for carrying out planning in intellectual disablities? Department of
    A. Education
    B. Welfare
    C. Labor
    D. Mental Hygiene

    6.____

7. Which one of the following publications dealt exclusively with intellectual disablity and related problems?
    A. THE VOLTA REVIEW
    B. THE TRAINING SCHOOL BULLETIN
    C. EXCEPTIONAL CHILDREN
    D. THE JOURNAL OF GENETIC PSYCHOLOGY

    7.____

8. *It is just as important to integrate the mentally retarded within our society and make full use of their abilities as it is to make a special effort to do this for the physically handicapped.*
   This statement was made by

   A. John F. Kennedy
   B. Lyndon B. Johnson
   C. Hubert Humphrey
   D. Dwight D. Eisenhower

9. The study of mental deficiency as a specialized branch of medicine did NOT develop until

   A. Itard demonstrated his success with the Wild Boy of Aveyron
   B. investigators realized that mental defect required treatment dissimilar to that of mental illness
   C. Goddard's work on the inheritance of mental defect was published
   D. Pinel removed the shackles from the patients at the Hospice des Bicetre

10. The *patterning* method of treating neurologically handicapped children was originated at the Institute

    A. of Neurological Diseases
    B. for the Achievement of Human Potential
    C. of Defectology
    D. for the Crippled and Disabled

11. Which one of the following may properly be considered the MOST significant recent development in rehabilitation of the intellectually disabled? The

    A. use of new diagnostic techniques with disabled young adults
    B. development of combined school-work programs
    C. use of rehabilitation counselors in the schools
    D. identification of social problems of the intellectually disabled

12. Which one of the following needs of the intellectually disabled is often minimized?

    A. Diagnosis
    B. Institutionalization
    C. Development of worthwhile leisure time activities
    D. Specially trained teachers

13. Which of the following is the MOST likely underlying cause of most vandalism in intellectually disabled school-age children?

    A. Compensation for feelings of helplessness
    B. Inadequate protection of property
    C. Delinquent or pre-delinquent personality structure
    D. Intra-gang competitiveness

14. Of the following, the developer of the *talking typewriter* used with disabled children was

    A. Samuel A. Kirk
    B. Albert J. Harris
    C. Paul A. Witty
    D. Omar K. Moore

15. The leaders in the national campaign to treat intellectual disablity recommend that the major responsibility for development of programs should be assumed by 15._____

    A. the federal government
    B. community agencies
    C. state governments
    D. municipal governments

16. A recent development in post-school vocational placement of the intellectually disabled is the assignment of the responsibility for placement to 16._____

    A. guidance counselors of the Board of Education's special education department
    B. community offices of the State Employment Service
    C. selective placement counselors of the Division of Vocational Rehabilitation
    D. special committees functioning within the parent organizations for the disabled

17. Which one of the following is a suitable industrial job operation for which a disabled high school student may be trained? 17._____

    A. Wire preparation and soldering
    B. Hot water boiler assembly
    C. Steamfitting
    D. Repair work on electric and gas driven lawnmowers

18. The PRIME objective of an educational program for the intellectually disabled should be the development of 18._____

    A. avocational pursuits and hobbies to fill their leisure time
    B. manipulative ability that will lead to some marketable skills
    C. reading skills that include the basic words in *reading for protection*
    D. general communication skills in both the school and the home

19. In a program of occupational education for the intellectually disabled, vocational guidance is interpreted as encompassing 19._____

    A. a study of appropriate jobs
    B. help for those with limited vocational potential to find jobs
    C. self-evaluation of individual qualifications against specific job requirements
    D. job placement

20. The average lifespan of an individual with Down syndrome is closest to 20._____

    A. 25　　　　B. 35　　　　C. 50　　　　D. 60

KEY (CORRECT ANSWERS)

1. D
2. D
3. A
4. D
5. A

6. D
7. B
8. A
9. B
10. B

11. B
12. C
13. A
14. D
15. C

16. B
17. A
18. D
19. C
20. D

TEST 2

DIRECTIONS: Each question or incomplete statement is followed by several suggested answers or completions. Select the one that BEST answers the question or completes the statement. *PRINT THE LETTER OF THE CORRECT ANSWER IN THE SPACE AT THE RIGHT.*

1. In this state, the period of compulsory school attendance for intellectually disabled children is

    A. the same as that for non-disabled children
    B. shorter than that for non-disabled children
    C. longer than that for non-disabled children
    D. either shorter or longer than that for non-disabled children, depending on the child's actual class progress

2. Recent publications from the federal government estimate the number of intellectually disabled people in the country to be APPROXIMATELY _____ million.

    A. 2.5   B. 6.5   C. 8.5   D. 11.5

3. A MOST significant legislative event relative to intellectual disablity was the passage of a law

    A. making it mandatory that all infants be tested for phenylketonuria
    B. subsidizing sheltered workshops on a per capita basis
    C. making it mandatory that emotionally disturbed children be provided with educational programs
    D. providing a salary differential for teachers of handicapped children

4. Which one of the following individuals exerted the GREATEST influence in the training of disabled children?

    A. Piaget   B. Montessori   C. Freud   D. Seguin

5. The incidence of intellectual disablity is

    A. greater among males than females
    B. greater among the offspring of the poor than the rich
    C. proportionally greater among Black than among white families
    D. greater among the offspring of uneducated than among offspring of educated families

6. The qualifying conditions for intellectual disablity for different age groups include social adjustment, learning ability, and rate of maturation.
Rate of maturation as a factor in intellectual disablity has special significance during the

    A. first few years of life
    B. primary school years
    C. adolescent period
    D. young adult period

7. Rubella may cause intellectual disablity when contracted by a pregnant woman, particularly during the

    A. first three months of pregnancy
    B. second three months of pregnancy
    C. third three months of pregnancy
    D. latter half of the pregnancy period

8. Studies of the relative abilities of disabled and normal individuals in learning indicate that the intellectually disabled

   A. show no difference in the rate or amount of learning compared to their normal peers of the same mental age
   B. are less capable in abstracting and generalizing from their experiences
   C. are not affected by the complexity of the task presented
   D. cannot be trained to use verbal cues in learning

9. Which one of the following phases of the Occupational Education program is NOT the responsibility of the teacher?

   A. Occupational information
   B. Vocational guidance
   C. Job placement
   D. Vocational training

10. A program of Occupational Education for the disabled adolescent places GREATEST emphasis upon the development of

    A. personal-social
    B. social-occupational
    C. occupational-academic
    D. academic-personal

11. In a program of Occupational Education for the intellectually disabled, vocational training should emphasize MOST heavily training in

    A. non-manual skills necessary in the work area
    B. general habits, attitudes, and skills common to good workmanship and citizenship
    C. manual skills needed in the work area
    D. measuring individual abilities against job requirements

12. In general, the HIGHEST job level at which an intellectually disabled individual can function in open competitive industry is as a(n)

    A. sheltered helper
    B. skilled worker
    C. semi-skilled worker
    D. unskilled worker

13. Which one of the following is the PRIMARY objective of the Work-Study program for intellectually disabled youth?

    A. Developing a realistic attitude toward school
    B. Determining the types of jobs they will be qualified to hold
    C. Emphasizing proper job attitudes
    D. Helping pupils make a successful transition from school to full-time employment

14. MOST maladoptive behavior of the intellectually disabled child is a function of his

    A. disablity
    B. interpersonal relationships
    C. academic frustrations
    D. faulty perception of the environment

15. The emotional problems exhibited by intellectually disabled children are essentially

    A. the same kind as those exhibited by non-disabled children
    B. dependent primarily upon the clinical classification of disablity
    C. determined by the child's constitutional endowment
    D. qualitatively different from those of children who are not disabled

16. The BEST single diagnostic index of disablity in a young pre-school child with normal visual and auditory capacities is   16.____

    A. an underdeveloped comprehension and speaking vocabulary for his age
    B. delayed motor development for his age
    C. inability to distinguish stimuli simultaneously presented to the face and hand
    D. an abnormal EEG record

17. According to Stanford-Binet, an IQ between 55 and 69 is _____ impaired or delayed.   17.____

    A. severely   B. moderately   C. mildly   D. average

18. Down syndrome is associated with   18.____

    A. head trauma   B. chromosomes   C. nutrition   D. infection

19. Which one of the following is MOST likely to be symptomatic of the defense mechanism known as *regression* in an older disabled child?   19.____

    A. Sudden immature behavior in a class
    B. Constant *forgetting* to do a class assignment
    C. Affirming that a dead parent is still alive
    D. Acting like another well-liked child in the class

20. To which one of the following therapeutic techniques is the use of role playing as a guidance tool MOST closely related?   20.____

    A. Group therapy   B. Free association
    C. Psychotherapy   D. Psychodrama

KEY (CORRECT ANSWERS)

1. A
2. B
3. A
4. D
5. A

6. A
7. A
8. B
9. C
10. B

11. B
12. C
13. D
14. B
15. A

16. A
17. C
18. B
19. A
20. D

PREPARING WRITTEN MATERIAL

I. COMMENTARY

The need to communicate-- clearly, swiftly, completely, effectively -- is basic to all organizations, agencies, departments --public and private, large and small.

Communication is accomplished by employing one or more of the accepted forms of communication, singly and/or together -- oral (verbal), written, visual, electronic, etc.

The method most often used to reach large numbers or groups of persons to achieve and ensure clarity, correctness, comprehension, uniformity, and permanence of effect, is through the preparation and issuance of written materials, e.g., notices, statements, letters, reports, descriptions, explanations, expositions, schedules, summaries, etc.

Preparing written material clearly and correctly is, therefore, a dutiable function of every regular and senior employee, foreman, supervisor, manager, administrator, director; and this quest ion-type is often used as a basic, integral part of various selection processes.

Questions involving correctness of expression usually appear on career written examinations as well as on other types of general tests.

While this question-type may take several forms, the two most usual presentations are the single-sentence type, which is to be evaluated as correct or incorrect on one of several bases, and the multiple-sentence type, involving four or five sentences, one of which is to be denoted as correct (or incorrect) for reasons of grammar and usage, or correctness of expression.

DIRECTIONS AND SAMPLE QUESTIONS

DIRECTIONS

Each of the sentences numbered I and II may be classified under one of the following four categories:
    A. *Faulty* because of incorrect grammar or word usage
    B. *Faulty* because of incorrect punctuation
    C. *Faulty* because of incorrect capitalization or incorrect spelling
    D. Correct

Examine each sentence carefully to determine under which of the above four options it is best classified. Then, in the space to the right, print the capital letter preceding the option which is the best of the four suggested above.

SAMPLE QUESTIONS

I. One of our clerks were promoted yesterday.   I.____

    The subject of this sentence is "one," so the verb should be "was promoted" instead of "were promoted." Since the sentence is incorrect because of bad grammar, the answer to Sample Question I Is (A)

II. Between you and me, I would prefer not going there.   II.____

    Since this sentence is correct, the answer to Sample Question II is (D)

PREPARING WRITTEN MATERIAL

II. COMMON ERRORS/CORRECT USES

Common Errors in Usage

1. being that for since
2. like for as
3. off of for-off
4. different than for different from
5. quick for quickly
6. careful for carefully
7. sure for surely
8. good for well
9. nothing for anything.
10. most for almost
11. real for really
12. this here for this
13. swell for excellent
14. well for good
15. those for that (kind)
16. less for fewer
17. them for those
18. they for he
19. him for he (after than)
20. their for his
21. who for whom
22. whom for who
23. I for me
24. are for is
25. tore for torn
26. wrote for-written
27. busted for burst
28. seen for saw
29. done for did
30. graduated for graduated from
31. irregardless for regardless
32. am living for have been living
33. laying for lying
34. leave for let
35. should of for should have
36. except for accept
37. besides for beside
38. affect for effect
39. amount for number
40. kind of a for kind of

Correct Usage

1. Since he was late, he was not admitted.
2. She smiles as her father does.
3. He took his hat off his head
4. Your pen is different from mine
5. Go quickly
6. He laid the tray down carefully.
7. The boy was surely happy to hear this.
8. I cannot hear well.
9. I didn't see anything.
10. Almost everyone was there.
11. The baby is really beautiful.
12. This ball is broken.
13. That was an excellent play.
14. She looks good in her new suit.
15. I prefer that kind of cigarettes.
16. We have fewer bad marks than they.
17. Please take those knives away.
18. People can be what they want to be.
19. I am younger than he.
20. Every soldier will do his duty.
21. Whom do you think I met today?
22. Who do you think it was?
23. Between you and me ...
24. Everybody is here
25. He had torn the manuscript in two.
26. I have written a play.
27. The bubble burst.
28. I saw the new boy.
29. He did it.
30. He graduated from Lincoln High.
31. Regardless of the weather, we will fly.
32. I have been living here for a month.
33. He was lying on the ground.
34. Let him go.
35. I should have thought of that.
36. I accept your apology.
37. I shall sit beside you.
38. The motion picture HOLOCAUST had a great effect on all who saw it.
39. We have a large number of books in the library.
40. What kind of car do you have?

PREPARING WRITTEN MATERIALS
EXAMINATION SECTION
TEST 1

DIRECTIONS: Each question consists of a sentence which may be classified appropriately under one of the following four categories:
- A. Incorrect because of faulty grammar or sentence structure.
- B. Incorrect because of faulty punctuation.
- C. Incorrect because of faulty spelling or capitalization.
- D. Correct

Examine each sentence carefully. Then, in the space at the right, print the capital letter preceding the option which is the BEST of the four suggested above. All incorrect sentences contain only one type of error. Consider a sentence correct if it contains none of the types of errors mentioned, although there may be other correct ways of expressing the same thought.

1. The fire apparently started in the storeroom, which is usually locked.   1.____

2. On approaching the victim two bruises were noticed by this officer.   2.____

3. The officer, who was there examined the report with great care.   3.____

4. Each employee in the office had a separate desk.   4.____

5. The suggested procedure is similar to the one now in use.   5.____

6. No one was more pleased with the new procedure than the chauffeur.   6.____

7. He tried to pursuade her to change the procedure.   7.____

8. The total of the expenses charged to petty cash were high.   8.____

9. An understanding between him and I was finally reached.   9.____

10. It was at the supervisor's request that the clerk agreed to postpone his vacation.   10.____

11. We do not believe that it is necessary for both he and the clerk to attend the conference.   11.____

12. All employees, who display perseverance, will be given adequate recognition.   12.____

13. He regrets that some of us employees are dissatisfied with our new assignments.   13.____

14. "Do you think that the raise was merited," asked the supervisor? 14.____

15. The new manual of procedure is a valuable supplament to our rules and regulation. 15.____

16. The typist admitted that she had attempted to pursuade the other employees to assist her in her work. 16.____

17. The supervisor asked that all amendments to the regulations be handled by you and I. 17.____

18. They told both he and I that the prisoner had escaped. 18.____

19. Any superior officer, who, disregards the just complaints of his subordinates, is remiss in the performance of his duty. 19.____

20. Only those members of the national organization who resided in the Middle west attended the conference in Chicago. 20.____

21. We told him to give the investigation assignment to whoever was available. 21.____

22. Please do not disappoint and embarass us by not appearing in court. 22.____

23. Despite the efforts of the Supervising mechanic, the elevator could not be started. 23.____

24. The U.S. Weather Bureau, weather record for the accident date was checked. 24.____

KEY (CORRECT ANSWERS)

1.	D	11.	A
2.	A	12.	B
3.	B	13.	D
4.	D	14.	B
5.	D	15.	C
6.	D	16.	C
7.	C	17.	A
8.	A	18.	A
9.	A	19.	B
10.	D	20.	C

21. D
22. C
23. C
24. B

TEST 2

DIRECTIONS: Each question consists of a sentence. Some of the sentences contain errors in English grammar or usage, punctuation, spelling, or capitalization. A sentence does not contain an error simply because it could be written in a different manner. Choose answer:
  A. If the sentence contains an error in English grammar or usage.
  B. if the sentence contains an error in punctuation.
  C. If the sentence contains an error in spelling or capitalization
  D. If the sentence does not contain any errors.

1. The severity of the sentence prescribed by contemporary statutes—including both the former and the revised New York Penal Laws—do not depend on what crime was intended by the offender.   1.____

2. It is generally recognized that two defects in the early law of attempt played a part in the birth of burglary: (1) immunity from prosecution for conduct short of the last act before completion of the crime, and (2) the relatively minor penalty imposed for an attempt (it being a common law misdemeanor) vis-à-vis the completed offense.   2.____

3. The first sentence of the statute is applicable to employees who enter their place of employment, invited guests, and all other persons who have an express or implied license or privilege to enter the premises.   3.____

4. Contemporary criminal codes in the United States generally divide burglary into various degrees, differentiating the categories according to place, time and other attendent circumstances.   4.____

5. The assignment was completed in record time but the payroll for it has not yet been prepaid.   5.____

6. The operator, on the other hand, is willing to learn me how to use the mimeograph.   6.____

7. She is the prettiest of the three sisters.   7.____

8. She doesn't know; if the mail has arrived.   8.____

9. The doorknob of the office door is broke.   9.____

10. Although the department's supply of scratch pads and stationery have diminished considerably, the allotment for our division has not been reduced.   10.____

11. You have not told us whom you wish to designate as your secretary.   11.____

12. Upon reading the minutes of the last meeting, the new proposal was taken up for consideration.   12.____

13. Before beginning the discussion, we locked the door as a precautionery measure.   13.____

14. The supervisor remarked, "Only those clerks, who perform routine work, are permitted to take a rest period."   14.____

15. Not only will this duplicating machine make accurate copies, but it will also produce a quantity of work equal to fifteen transcribing typists.   15.____

16. "Mr. Jones," said the supervisor, "we regret our inability to grant you an extention of your leave of absence."   16.____

17. Although the employees find the work monotonous and fatigueing, they rarely complain.   17.____

18. We completed the tabulation of the receipts on time despite the fact that Miss Smith our fastest operator was absent for over a week.   18.____

19. The reaction of the employees who attended the meeting, as well as the reaction of those who did not attend, indicates clearly that the schedule is satisfactory to everyone concerned.   19.____

20. Of the two employees, the one in our office is the most efficient.   20.____

21. No one can apply or even understand, the new rules and regulations.   21.____

22. A large amount of supplies were stored in the empty office.   22.____

23. If an employee is occassionally asked to work overtime, he should do so willingly.   23.____

24. It is true that the new procedures are difficult to use but, we are certain that you will learn them quickly.   24.____

25. The office manager said that he did not know who would be given a large allotment under the new plan.   25.____

KEY (CORRECT ANSWERS)

1. A
2. D
3. D
4. C
5. C

6. A
7. D
8. B
9. A
10. A

11. D
12. A
13. C
14. B
15. A

16. C
17. C
18. B
19. D
20. A

21. B
22. A
23. C
24. B
25. D

TEST 3

DIRECTIONS: Each of the following sentences may be classified MOST appropriately under one of the following categories:
- A. Faulty because of incorrect grammar
- B. Faulty because of incorrect punctuation
- C. Faulty because of incorrect capitalization
- D. Correct

Examine each sentence carefully. Then, in the space at the right, print the capital letter preceding the option which is the BEST of the four suggested above. All incorrect sentence contain but one type of error. Consider a sentence correct if it contains none of the types of errors mentioned, even though there may be other correct ways of expressing the same thought.

1. The desk, as well as the chairs, were moved out of the office. 1._____

2. The clerk whose production was greatest for the month won a day's vacation as first prize. 2._____

3. Upon entering the room, the employees were found hard at work at their desks. 3._____

4. John Smith our new employee always arrives at work on time. 4._____

5. Punish whoever is guilty of stealing the money. 5._____

6. Intelligent and persistent effort lead to success no matter what the job may be. 6._____

7. The secretary asked, "can you call again at three o'clock?" 7._____

8. He told us, that if the report was not accepted at the next meeting, it would have to be rewritten. 8._____

9. He would not have sent the letter if he had known that it would cause so much excitement. 9._____

10. We all looked forward to him coming to visit us. 10._____

11. If you find that you are unable to complete the assignment please notify me as soon as possible. 11._____

12. Every girl in the office went home on time but me; there was still some work for me to finish. 12._____

13. He wanted to know who the letter was addressed to, Mr. Brown or Mr. Smith. 13._____

14. "Mr. Jones, he said, please answer this letter as soon as possible." 14._____

15. The new clerk had an unusual accent inasmuch as he was born and educated in the south. 15.____

16. Although he is younger than her, he earns a higher salary. 16.____

17. Neither of the two administrators are going to attend the conference being held in Washington, D.C. 17.____

18. Since Miss Smith and Miss Jones have more experience than us, they have been given more responsible duties. 18.____

19. Mr. Shaw the supervisor of the stock room maintains an inventory of stationery and office supplies. 19.____

20. Inasmuch as this matter affects both you and I, we should take joint action. 20.____

21. Who do you think will be able to perform this highly technical work? 21.____

22. Of the two employees, John is considered the most competent. 22.____

23. He is not coming home on tuesday; we expect him next week. 23.____

24. Stenographers, as well as typists must be able to type rapidly and accurately. 24.____

25. Having been placed in the safe we were sure that the money would not be stolen. 25.____

KEY (CORRECT ANSWERS)

1.	A	11.	B
2.	D	12.	D
3.	A	13.	A
4.	B	14.	B
5.	D	15.	C
6.	A	16.	A
7.	C	17.	A
8.	B	18.	A
9.	D	19.	B
10.	A	20.	A

21. D
22. A
23. C
24. B
25. A

TEST 4

DIRECTIONS: Each of the following sentences consist of four sentences lettered A, B, C, and D. One of the sentences in each group contains an error in grammar or punctuation. Indicate the INCORRECT sentence in each group. *PRINT THE LETTER OF THE CORRECT ANSWER IN THE SPACE AT THE RIGHT.*

1. A. Give the message to whoever is on duty.
    B. The teacher who's pupil won first prize presented the award.
    C. Between you and me, I don't expect the program to succeed.
    D. His running to catch the bus caused the accident.

    1.____

2. A. The process, which was patented only last year is already obsolete.
    B. His interest in science (which continues to the present) led him to convert his basement into a laboratory.
    C. He described the book as "verbose, repetitious, and bombastic".
    D. Our new director will need to possess three qualities: vision, patience, and fortitude.

    2.____

3. A. The length of ladder trucks varies considerably.
    B. The probationary fireman reported to the officer to who he was assigned.
    C. The lecturer emphasized the need for we firemen to be punctual.
    D. Neither the officers nor the members of the company knew about the new procedure.

    3.____

4. A. Ham and eggs is the specialty of the house.
    B. He is one of the students who are on probation.
    C. Do you think that either one of us have a chance to be nominated for president of the class?
    D. I assume that either he was to be in charge or you were.

    4.____

5. A. Its a long road that has no turn.
    B. To run is more tiring than to walk.
    C. We have been assigned three new reports: namely, the statistical summary, the narrative summary, and the budgetary summary.
    D. Had the first payment been made in January, the second would be due in April.

    5.____

6. A. Each employer has his own responsibilities.
    B. If a person speaks correctly, they make a good impression.
    C. Every one of the operators has had her vacation.
    D. Has anybody filed his report?

    6.____

7. A. The manager, with all his salesmen, was obliged to go.
    B. Who besides them is to sign the agreement?
    C. One report without the others is incomplete.
    D. Several clerks, as well as the proprietor, was injured.

    7.____

8. A. A suspension of these activities is expected.
    B. The machine is economical because first cost and upkeep are low.
    C. A knowledge of stenography and filing are required for this position.
    D. The condition in which the goods were received shows that the packing was not done properly.

9. A. There seems to be a great many reasons for disagreement.
    B. It does not seem possible that they could have failed.
    C. Have there always been too few applicants for these positions?
    D. There is no excuse for these errors.

10. A. We shall be pleased to answer your question.
    B. Shall we plan the meeting for Saturday?
    C. I will call you promptly at seven.
    D. Can I borrow your book after you have read it?

11. A. You are as capable as I.
    B. Everyone is willing to sign but him and me.
    C. As for he and his assistant, I cannot praise them too highly.
    D. Between you and me, I think he will be dismissed.

12. A. Our competitors bid above us last week.
    B. The survey which was began last year has not yet been completed.
    C. The operators had shown that they understood their instructions.
    D. We have never ridden over worse roads.

13. A. Who did they say was responsible?
    B. Whom did you suspect?
    C. Who do you suppose it was?
    D. Whom do you mean?

14. A. Of the two propositions, this is the worse.
    B. Which report do you consider the best—the one in January or the one in July?
    C. I believe this is the most practicable of the many plans submitted.
    D. He is the youngest employee in the organization.

15. A. The firm had but three orders last week.
    B. That doesn't really seem possible.
    C. After twenty years scarcely none of the old business remains.
    D. Has he done nothing about it?

KEY (CORRECT ANSWERS)

1.	B	6.	B	11.	C
2.	A	7.	D	12.	B
3.	C	8.	C	13.	A
4.	C	9.	A	14.	B
5.	A	10.	D	15.	C

PREPARING WRITTEN MATERIAL

PARAGRAPH REARRANGEMENT
COMMENTARY

The sentences that follow are in scrambled order. You are to rearrange them in proper order and indicate the letter choice containing the correct answer at the space at the right.

Each group of sentences in this section is actually a paragraph presented in scrambled order. Each sentence in the group has a place in that paragraph; no sentence is to be left out. You are to read each group of sentences and decide upon the best order in which to put the sentences so as to form a well-organized paragraph.

The questions in this section measure the ability to solve a problem when all the facts relevant to its solution are not given.

More specifically, certain positions of responsibility and authority require the employee to discover connection between events sometimes, apparently, unrelated. In order to do this, the employee will find it necessary to correctly infer that unspecified events have probably occurred or are likely to occur. This ability becomes especially important when action must be taken on incomplete information.

Accordingly, these questions require competitors to choose among several suggested alternatives, each of which presents a different sequential arrangement of the events. Competitors must choose the MOST logical of the suggested sequences.

In order to do so, they may be required to draw on general knowledge to infer missing concepts or events that are essential to sequencing the given events. Competitors should be careful to infer only what is essential to the sequence. The plausibility of the wrong alternatives will always require the inclusion of unlikely events or of additional chains of events which are NOT essential to sequencing the given events.

It's very important to remember that you are looking for the best of the four possible choices, and that the best choice of all may not even be one of the answers you're given to choose from.

There is no one right way to solve these problems. Many people have found it helpful to first write out the order of the sentences, as they would have arranged them, on their scrap paper before looking at the possible answers. If their optimum answer is there, this can save them some time. If it isn't, this method can still give insight into solving the problem. Others find it most helpful to just go through each of the possible choices, contrasting each as they go along. You should use whatever method feels comfortable and works for you.

While most of these types of questions are not that difficult, we've added a higher percentage of the difficult type, just to give you more practice. Usually there are only one or two questions on this section that contain such subtle distinctions that you're unable to answer confidently. And you then may find yourself stuck deciding between two possible choices, neither of which you're sure about.

PREPARING WRITTEN MATERIAL
PARAGRAPH REARRANGEMENT
EXAMINATION SECTION
TEST 1

DIRECTIONS: The following groups of sentences need to be arranged in an order that makes sense. Select the letter preceding the sequence that represents the best sentence order. *PRINT THE LETTER OF THE CORRECT ANSWER IN THE SPACE AT THE RIGHT.*

1. I. The ostrich egg shell's legendary toughness makes it an excellent substitute for certain types of dishes or dinnerware, and in parts of Africa ostrich shells are cut and decorated for use as containers for water.
    II. Since prehistoric times, people have used the enormous egg of the ostrich as a part of their diet, a practice which has required much patience and hard work—to hard boil an ostrich egg takes about four hours.
    III. Opening the egg's shell, which is rock hard and nearly an inch thick, requires heavy tools, such as a saw or chisel; from inside, a baby ostrich must use a hornlike projection on its beak as a miniature pick-axe to escape from the egg.
    IV. The offspring of all higher-order animals originate from single egg cells that are carried by mothers, and most of these eggs are relatively small, often microscopic.
    V. The egg of the African ostrich, however, weighs a massive thirty pounds, making it the largest single cell on earth, and a common object of human curiosity and wonder.
    The BEST order is:
    A. V, IV, I, II, III   B. I, IV, V, III, II   C. IV, II, III, V, I   D. IV, V, II, III, I

    1.____

2. I. Typically only a few feet high on the open sea, individual tsunami have been known to circle the entire globe two or three times if their progress is not interrupted, but are not usually dangerous until they approach the shallow water that surrounds land masses.
    II. Some of the most terrifying and damaging hazards caused by earthquakes are tsunami, which were once called "tidal waves"—a poorly chosen name, since these waves have nothing to do with tides.
    III. Then a wave, slowed by the sudden drag on the lower part of its moving water column, will pile upon itself, sometimes reaching a height of over 100 feet.
    IV. Tsunami (Japanese for "great harbor wave") are seismic waves that are caused by earthquakes near oceanic trenches, and once triggered, can travel up to 600 miles an hour on the open ocean.
    V. A land-shoaling tsunami is capable of extraordinary destruction; some tsunami have deposited large boats miles inland, washed out two-foot-thick seawalls, and scattered locomotive trains over long distances.
    The BEST order is:
    A. IV, I, III, II, V   B. I, III, IV, II, V   C. V, I, III, II, IV   D. II, IV, I, III, V

    2.____

3.
  I. Soon, by the 1940s, jazz was the most popular type of music among American intellectuals and college students.
  II. In the early days of jazz, it was considered "lowdown" music, or music that was played only in rough, disreputable bars and taverns.
  III. However, jazz didn't take too long to develop from early ragtime melodies into more complex, sophisticated forms, such as Charlie Parker's "bebop" style of jazz.
  IV. After charismatic band leaders such as Duke Ellington and Count Basie brought jazz to a larger audience, and jazz continued to evolve into more complicated forms, white audiences began to accept and even to enjoy the new American art form.
  V. Many white Americans, who then dictated the tastes of society, were wary of music that was played almost exclusively in black clubs in the poorer sections of cities and towns.

  The BEST order is:
  A. V, IV, III, II, I   B. II, V, III, IV, I   C. IV, V, III, I, II   D. I, II, IV, III, V

3._____

4.
  I. Then, hanging in a windless place, the magnetized end of the needle would always point to the south.
  II. The needle could then be balanced on the rim of a cup, or the edge of a fingernail, but this balancing act was hard to maintain, and the needle often fell off.
  III. Other needles would point to the north, and it was important for any traveler finding his way with a compass to remember which kind of magnetized needle he was carrying.
  IV. To make some of the earliest compasses in recorded history, ancient Chinese "magicians" would rub a needle with a piece of magnetized iron called a lodestone.
  V. A more effective method of keeping the needle free to swing with its magnetic pull was to attach a strand of silk to the center of the needle with a tiny piece of wax.

  The BEST order is:
  A. IV, II, V, I, III   B. IV, III, V, II, I   C. IV, V, II, I, III   D. IV, I, III, V, II

4._____

5.
  I. The now-famous first mate of the *H.M.S. Bounty*, Fletcher Christian, founded one of the world's most peculiar civilizations in 1790.
  II. The men knew they had just committed a crime for which they could be hanged, so they set sail for Pitcairn, a remote, abandoned island in the far eastern region of the Polynesian archipelago, accompanied by twelve Polynesian women and six men.
  III. In a mutiny that has become legendary, Christian and the others forced Captain Bligh into a lifeboat and set him adrift off the coast of Tonga in April of 1789.
  IV. In early 1790, the *Bounty* landed at Pitcairn Island, where the men lived out the rest of their lives and founded an isolated community which to this day includes direct descendants of Christian and the other Crewmen.

5._____

V. The *Bounty*, commanded by Captain William Bligh, was in the middle of a global voyage, and Christian and his shipmates had come to the conclusion that Bligh was a reckless madman who would lead them to their deaths unless they took the ship from him.

The BEST order is:
A. IV, V, III, II, I   B. I, III, V, II, IV   C. I, V, III, II, IV   D. III, I, V, IV, II

6.
I. But once the vines had been led to make orchids, the flowers had to be carefully hand-pollinated, because unpollinated orchids usually lasted less than a day, wilting and dropping off the vine before it had even become dark.
II. The Totonac farmers discovered that looping a vine back around once it reached a five-foot height on its host tree would cause the vine to flower.
III. Though they knew how to process the fruit pods and extract vanilla's flavoring agent, the Totonacs also knew that a wild vanilla vine did not produce abundant flowers or fruit.
IV. Wild vines climbed along the trunks and canopies of trees, and this constant upward growth diverted most of the vine's energy to making leaves instead of the orchid flowers that once pollinated, would produce the flavorful pods.
V. Hundreds of years before vanilla became a prized food flavoring in Europe and the Western World, the Totonac Indians of the Mexican Gulf Coast were skilled cultivators of the vanilla vine, whose fruit they literally worshipped as a goddess.

The BEST order is:
A. II, III, IV, I, V   B. II, IV, III, I, V   C. V, III, IV, II, I   D. III, IV, I, II, V

6.____

7.
I. Once airborne, the spider is at the mercy of the air currents—usually the spider takes a brief journey, traveling close to the ground, but some have been found in air samples collected as high as 10,000 feet, or been reported landing on ships far out at sea.
II. Once a young spider has hatched, it must leave the environment into which it was born as quickly as possible, in order to avoid competing with its hundreds of brothers and sisters for food.
III. The silk rises into warm air currents, and as soon as the pull feels adequate the spider lets go and drifts up into the air, suspended from the silk strand in the same way that a person might parasail.
IV. To help young spiders do this, many species have adapted a practice known as "aerial dispersal," or, in common speech, "ballooning."
V. A spider that wants to leave its surroundings quickly will climb to the top of a grass system or twig, face into the wind, and aim its back end into the air, releasing a long stream of silk from the glands near the tip of its abdomen.

The BEST order is:
A. V, IV, II, III, I   B. V, II, IV, I, III   C. II, V, IV, III, I   D. II, IV, V, III, I

7.____

8. I. For about a year, Tycho worked at a castle in Prague with a scientist named Johannes Kepler, but their association was cut short by another argument that drove Kepler out of the castle, to later develop, on his own, the theory of planetary orbits.
   II. Tycho found life without a nose embarrassing, so he made a new nose for himself out of silver, which reportedly remained glued to his face for the rest of his life.
   III. Tycho Brahe, the 17th-century Danish astronomer, is today more famous for his odd and arrogant personality than for any contribution he has made to our knowledge of the stars and planets.
   IV. Early in his career, as a student at Rostock University, Tycho got into an argument with another student about who was the better mathematician, and the two became so angry that the argument turned into a sword fight, during which Tycho's nose was sliced off.
   V. Later in his life, Tycho's arrogance may have kept him from playing a part in one of the greatest astronomical discoveries in history: the elliptical orbits of the solar system's planets.
   The BEST order is:
   A. I, IV, II, III, V   B. IV, II, III, V, I   C. IV, II, I, III, V   D. III, IV, II, V, I

9. I. The processionaries are so used to this routine that if a person picks up the end of a silk line and brings it back to the origin—creating a closed circle—the caterpillars may travel around and around for days, sometimes starving or freezing, without changing course.
   II. Rather than relying on sight or sound, the other caterpillars, who are lined up end-to-end behind the leader, travel to and from their nests by walking on this silk line, and each will reinforce it by laying down its own marking line as it passes over.
   III. In order to insure the safety of individuals, the processionary caterpillar nests in a tree with dozens of other caterpillars, and at night, when it is safest, they all leave together in search of food.
   IV. The processionary caterpillar of the European continent is a perfect illustration of how much some inspect species rely on instinct in their daily routines.
   V. As they leave their nests, the processionaries form a single-file line behind a leader who spins and lays out a silk line to mark the chosen path.
   The BEST order is:
   A. IV, III, V, II, I   B. III, V, IV, II, I   C. III, V, II, I, IV   D. IV, V, III, I, II

10. I. Often, the child is also given a handcrafted walker or push cart, to provide support for its first upright explorations.
    II. In traditional Indian families, a child's first steps are celebrated as a ceremonial event, rooted in ancient myth.
    III. These carts are often intricately designed to resemble the chariot of Krishna, an important figure in Indian mythology.
    IV. The sound of these anklet bells is intended to mimic the footsteps of the legendary child Rama, who is celebrated in devotional songs throughout India.

V. When the child's parents see that the child is ready to begin walking, they will fit it with specially designed ankle bracelets, adorned with gently ringing bells.

The BEST order is:
A. II, III, IV, I, V   B. II, V, III, I, IV   C. V, IV, I, III, II   D. V, III, II, I, IV

11. I. The settlers planted Osage oranges all across Middle America, and today long lines and rectangles of Osage orange trees can still be seen on the prairies, running along the former boundaries of farms that no longer exist.
II. After trying sod walls and water-filled ditches with no success, American farmers began to look for a plant that was adaptable to prairie weather, and that could be trimmed into a hedge that was "pig-tight, horse-high, and bull-strong."
III. The tree, so named because it bore a large (but inedible) fruit the size of an orange, was among the sturdiest and hardiest of American trees, and was prized among Native Americans for the strength and flexibility of bows which were made from its wood.
IV. The first people to practice agriculture on the American flatlands were faced with an important problem: what would they use to fence their land in a place that was almost entirely without trees or rocks?
V. Finally, an Illinois farmer brought the settlers a tree that was native to the land between the Red and Arkansas rivers, a tree called the Osage orange.

The BEST order is:
A. II, I, V, III, IV   B. I, II, III, IV, V   C. IV, II, V, III, I   D. IV, II, I, III, V

11.____

12. I. After about ten minutes of such spirited and complicated activity, the head dancer is free to make up his or her own movements while maintaining the interest of the New Year's crowd.
II. The dancer will then perform a series of leg kicks, while at the same time operating the lion's mouth with his own hand and moving the ears and eyes by means of a string which is attached to the dancer's own mouth.
III. The most difficult role of this dance belongs to the one who controls the lion's head; this person must lead all the other "parts" of the lion through the choreographed segments of the dance.
IV. The head dancer begins with a complex series of steps. alternately stepping forward with the head raised, and then retreating a few steps while lowering the head, a movement that is intended to create the impression that the lion is keeping a watchful eye for anything evil.
V. When performing a traditional Chinese New Year's lion dance, several performers must fit themselves inside a large lion costume and work together to enact different parts of the dance.

The BEST order is:
A. V, III, IV, II, I   B. III, IV, II, V, I   C. III, I, V, IV, II   D. IV, II, III, V, I

12.____

13. I.   For many years the shell of the chambered nautilus was treasured in Europe for its beauty and intricacy, but collectors were unaware that they were in possession of the structure that marked a "missing link" in the evolution of marine mollusks.
     II. The nautilus, however, evolved a series of enclosed chambers in its shell, and invented a new use for the structure: the shell began to serve as a buoyancy device.
     III. Equipped with this new flotation device, the nautilus did not need the single, muscular foot of its predecessors, but instead developed flaps, tentacles, and a gentle form of jet propulsion that transformed it into the first mollusk able to take command of its own density and explore a three-dimensional world.
     IV. By pumping and adjusting air pressure into the chambers, the nautilus could spend the day resting on the bottom, and then rise toward the surface at night in search of food.
     V.   The nautilus shell looks like a large snail shell, similar to those of its ancestors, who used their shells as protective coverings while they were anchored to the sea floor.

     The BEST order is:
     A. V, II, IV, I, III   B. V, I, II, III, IV   C. I, II, V, III, IV   D. I, V, II, IV, III

13.____

14. I.   While France and England battled for control of the region, the Acadiens prospered on the fertile farmland, which was finally secured by England in 1713.
     II. Early in the 17th century, settlers from Western France founded a colony called Acadie in what is now the Canadian province of Nova Scotia.
     III. At this time, English officials feared the presence of spies among the Acadiens who might be loyal to their French homeland, and the Acadiens were deported to spots along the Atlantic and Caribbean shores of America.
     IV. The French settlers remained on this land, under English rule, for around forty years, until the beginning of the French and Indian War, another conflict between France and England.
     V.   As the Acadien refugees drifted toward a final home in Southern Louisiana, neighbors shortened their name to "Cadien," and finally "Cajun," the name which the descendants of early Acadiens still call themselves.

     The BEST order is:
     A. I, IV, II, III, V   B. II, I, III, V, IV   C. II, I, IV, III, V   D. V, II, III, IV, I

14.____

15. I.   Traditional households in the Eastern and Western regions of Africa serve two meals a day—one at around noon, and the other in the evening.
     II. The starch is then used in the way that Americans might use a spoon, to scoop up a portion of the main dish on the person's plate.
     III. The reason for the starch's inclusion in every meal has to do with taste as well as nutrition; African food can be very spicy, and the starch is known to cool the burning effect of the main dish.
     IV. When serving these meals, the main dish is usually served on individual plates, and the starch is served on a communal plate, from which diners break off a piece of bread or scoop rice or fufu in their fingers.

15.____

V. The typical meals usually consist of a thick stew or soup as the main course, and an accompanying starch—either bread, rice, or *fufu*, a starchy grain paste similar in consistency to mashed potatoes.

The BEST order is:
A. V, II, III, IV, I B. V, I, IV, III, II C. I, IV, V, III, II D. I, V, IV, II, III

16. I. In the early days of the American Midwest, Indiana settlers sometimes came together to hold an event called an apple peeling, where neighboring settlers gathered at the homestead of a host family to help prepare the hosts' apple crop for cooking, canning, and making apple butter.
 II. At the beginning of the event, each peeler sat down in front of a ten- or twenty-gallon stone jar and was given a crock of apples and a paring knife.
 III. Once a peeler had finished with a crock, another was placed next to him; if the peeler was an unmarried man, he kept a strict count of the number of apples he had peeled, because the winner was allowed to kiss the girl of his choice.
 IV. The peeling usually ended by 9:30 in the evening, when the neighbors gathered in the host family's parlor for a dance social.
 V. The apples were peeled, cored, and quartered, and then placed into the jar.

The BEST order is:
A. I, V, III, IV, II B. II, V, III, IV, I C. I, II, V, III, IV D. II, I, V, IV, III

16.____

17. I. If your pet turtle is a land turtle and is native to temperate climates, it will stop eating some time in October, which should be your cue to prepare the turtle for hibernation.
 II. The box should then be covered with a wire screen, which will protect the turtle from any rodents or predators that might want to take advantage of a motionless and helpless animal.
 III. When your turtle hasn't eaten for a while and appears ready to hibernate, it should be moved to its winter quarters, most likely a cellar or garage, where the temperature should range between 40° and 45°F.
 IV. Instead of feeding the turtle, you should bathe it every day in warm water, to encourage the turtle to empty its intestines in preparation for its long winter sleep.
 V. Here the turtle should be placed in a well-ventilated box whose bottom is covered with a moisture-absorbing layer of clay beads, and then filled three-fourths full with almost dry peat moss or wood chips, into which the turtle will burrow and sleep for several months.

The BEST order is:
A. I, IV, III, V, II B. III, IV, II, V, I C. III, II, IV, I, V D. IV, V, II, III, I

17.____

18. I. Once he has reached the nest, the hunter uses two sturdy bamboo poles like huge chopsticks to pull the next away from the mountainside, into a large basket that will be lowered to people waiting below.
 II. The world's largest honeybees colonize the Nealese mountainsides, building honeycombs as large as a person on sheer rock faces that are often hundreds of feet high.

18.____

III. In the remote mountain country of Nepal, a small band of "honey hunters" carry out a tradition so ancient that 10,000 year-old drawings of the practice have been found in the caves of Nepal.
IV. To harvest the honey and beeswax from these combs, a honey hunter climbs above the nests, lowers a long bamboo-fiber ladder over the cliff, and then climbs down.
V. Throughout this dangerous practice, the hunter is stung repeatedly, and only the veterans, with skin that has been toughened over the years, are able to return from a hunt without the painful swelling caused by stings.

The BEST order is:
A. II, IV, III, V, I   B. II, IV, I, V, III   C. V, III, II, IV, I   D. III, II, IV, I, V

19. I. After the Romans left Britain, there were relentless attacks on the islands from the barbarian tribes of northern Germany—the Angles, Saxons, and Jutes.
II. As the empire weakened, Roman soldiers withdrew from Britain, leaving behind a country that continued to practice the Christian religion that had been introduced by the Romans.
III. Early Latin writings tell of a Christian warrior named Arturius (Arthur, in English) who led the British citizens to defeat these barbarian invades, and brought an extended period of peace to the lands of Britain.
IV. Long ago, the British Isles were part of the far-flung Roman Empire that extended across most of Europe and into Africa and Asia.
V. The romantic legend of King Arthur and his knights of the Round Table, one of the most popular and widespread stories of all time, appears to have some foundation in history.

The BEST order is:
A. V, IV, III, II, I   B. V, IV, II, I, III   C. IV, V, II, III, I   D. IV, III, II, I, V

19.____

20. I. The cylinder was allowed to cool until it could stand on its own, and then it was cut from the tube and split down the side with a single straight cut.
II. Nineteenth-century glassmakers, who had not yet discovered the glazier's modern techniques for making panes of glass, had to create a method for converting their blown gas into flat sheets.
III. The bubble was then pierced at the end to make a hole that opened up while the glassmaker gently spun it, creating a cylinder of glass.
IV. Turned on its side and laid on a conveyor belt, the cylinder was strengthened, or tempered, by being heated again and cooled very slowly, eventually flattening out into a single rectangular of glass.
V. To do this, the glassmaker dipped the end of a long tube into melted glass and blew into the other end of the tube, creating an expanding bubble of glass.

The BEST order is:
A. II, V, III, IV, I   B. II, IV, V, III, I   C. III, V, II, IV, I   D. III, I, IV, V, II

20.____

21.
I. The splints are almost always hidden, but horses are occasionally born whose splinted toes project from the leg on either side, just above the hoof.
II. The second and fourth toes remained, but shrank to thin splints of bone that fused invisibly to the horse's leg bone.
III. Horses are unique among mammals, having evolved feet that each end in what is essentially a single toe, capped by a large, sturdy hoof.
IV. Julius Caesar, an emperor of ancient Rome, was said to have owned one of these three-toed horses, and considered it so special that he would not permit anyone else to ride it.
V. Though the horse's earlier ancestors possessed the traditional mammalian set of five toes on each foot, the horse has retained only its third toe; its first and fifth toes disappeared completely as the horse evolved.
The BEST order is:
  A. III, V, II, I, IV   B. V, III, II, IV, I   C. III, II, V, I, IV   D. V, II, III, I, IV

22.
I. The new building materials—some of which are twenty feet long, and weigh nearly six tons—were transported to Pohnpei on rafts, and were brought into their present position by using hibiscus fiber ropes and leverage to move the stone columns upward along the inclined trunks of coconut palm trees.
II. The ancestors built great fires to heat the stone, and then poured cool seawater on the columns, which caused the stone to contract and split along natural fracture lines.
III. The now-abandoned enclave of Nan Madol, a group of 92 man-made islands off the shore of the Micronesian island of Pohnpei, is estimated to have been built around the year 500 A.D.
IV. The islanders say their ancestors quarried stone columns from a nearby island, where large basalt columns were formed by the cooling of molten lava.
V. The structures of Nan Madol are remarkable for the sheer size of some of the stone "longs" or columns that were used to create the walls of the offshore community, and today anthropologists can only rely on the information of existing local people for clues about how Nan Madol was built.
The BEST order is:
  A. V, IV, III, II, I   B. V, III, I, IV, II   C. III, V, IV, II, I   D. III, I, IV, II, V

23.
I. One of the most easily manipulated substances on earth, glass can be made into ceramic tiles that are composed of over 90% air.
II. NASA's space shuttles are the first spacecraft ever designed to leave and re-enter the earth's atmosphere while remaining intact.
III. These ceramic tiles are such effective insulators that when a tile emerges from the oven in which it was fired, it can be held safely in a person's hand by the edges while its interior still glows at a temperature well over 2000°F.
IV. Eventually, the engineers were led to a material that is as old as our most ancient civilization.
V. Because the temperature during atmospheric re-entry is so incredibly hot, it took NASA's engineers some time to find a substance capable of protecting the shuttles.

The BEST order is:

A. V, II, I, II, IV   B. II, V, IV, I, III   C. II, III, I, IV, V   D. V, IV, III, I, II

24. I. The secret to teaching any parakeet to talk is patience, and the understanding that when a bird talks," it is simply imitating what it hears, rather than putting ideas into words.
    II. You should stay just out of sight of the bird and repeat the phrase you want it to learn, for at least fifteen minutes every morning and evening.
    III. It is important to leave the bird without any words of encouragement or farewell; otherwise it might combine stray remarks or phrases, such as "Good night," with the phrase you are trying to teach it.
    IV. For this reason, to train your bird to imitate your words you should keep it free of any distractions, especially other noises, while you are giving it "lesson."
    V. After your repetition, you should quietly leave the bird alone for a while, to think over what it has just heard.

    The BEST order is:

    A. I, IV, II, V, III   B. I, II, IV, III, V   C. III, II, I, V, IV   D. III, I, V, IV, II

24.____

25. I. As a school approaches, fishermen from neighboring communities join their fishing boats together as a fleet, and string their gill nets together to make a huge fence that is held up by cork floats.
    II. At a signal from the party leaders, or *nakura*, the family members pound the sides of the boats or beat the water with long poles, creating a sudden and deafening noise.
    III. The fishermen work together to drag the trap into a half-circle that may reach 300 yards in diameter, and then the families move their boats to form the other half of the circle around the school of fish.
    IV. The school of fish flee from the commotion into the awaiting trap, where a final wall of net is thrown over the open end of the half-circle, securing the day's haul.
    V. Indonesian people from the area around the Sulu islands live on the sea, in floating villages made of lashed-together or stilted homes, and make much of their living by fishing their home waters for migrating schools of snapper, scad, and other fish.

    The BEST order is:

    A. I, V, III, IV, II   B. I, II, IV, III, V   C. V, I, II, III, IV   D. V, I, III, II, IV

25.____

KEY (CORRECT ANSWERS)

1.	D	11.	C
2.	D	12.	A
3.	B	13.	D
4.	A	14.	C
5.	C	15.	D
6.	C	16.	C
7.	D	17.	A
8.	D	18.	D
9.	A	19.	B
10.	B	20.	A

21. A
22. C
23. B
24. A
25. D

Sample Test Material for:

THE IN-BASKET

Test material will be presented in a job simulation exercise format.

For more information about this format, please see the section titled *More Information on Job Simulation Exercises* that follows the Sample Job Simulation Exercise.

Test Task: You will be given **Background** information on a fictional agency and your role in the agency. You will then be presented with a series of situations. Each situation will be followed by a list of choices that represent possible responses one could make. You will need to read the information presented and select the best choice(s) to take to collect relevant information and/or resolve the problem(s) in the situation described.

SAMPLE JOB SIMULATION EXERCISE:

Background and Sections A and B:

BACKGROUND

A new bureau, the **Bureau of Communications,** has just been organized within the Department of Regulations. The Bureau Director is Rena Morgan. The Bureau's principal objective is the efficient and effective flow of communication and information within and among divisions in the Department and between the Department and its publics.

The **Bureau of Communications** is comprised of three groups:

- The **Public Relations Group** serves as the liaison between the Department's Commissioner and Executive Office, and the public -- primarily the media.
- The **Freedom of Information Group** maintains and processes requests from individuals and groups for information under the Freedom of Information Laws and Regulations.
- The **Central Communications Group** serves as an information and communication center for Department management and the general public.

You have recently been appointed as Head of the Central Communications Group within the Bureau of Communications. The principal functions and activities of your group are as follows:

- Make and coordinate presentations on Department issues to the public and other interest groups.
- Respond to letters and telephone inquiries on general issues pertinent to Department operations.
- Serve as liaison between the Department and Legislative staff.
- Produce Department publications.
- Design Department forms for public and internal use.
- Prepare Department annual report and other reports as assigned.
- Assist Public Relations Group staff with publicity issues.
- Review communication flow within the Department and recommend necessary improvements.
- Assist in drafting and disseminating Department policies and procedures.

Your supervisor is Rena Morgan, Director, Bureau of Communications.

As Head of the Central Communications Group, you supervise a secretary and three unit supervisors:

- Sandra Fineberg, Secretary 1
- Frank Williams, Supervisor, Agency Publication Unit
- Mary Walters, Supervisor, Agency Presentations Unit
- Bill Richards, Supervisor, Legislative Inquiries Unit

Frank Williams and Mary Walters are both experienced employees. Frank and Mary each supervise two professional staff. Bill Richards has recently been assigned to your group after spending the first 18 months of his agency employment in one of the Department's line divisions. Bill's unit has one professional staff position, which is currently vacant. In addition to working as your secretary, Sandra Fineberg also provides word processing support to Frank, Mary, and Bill and their unit staff.

You have been Head of the Central Communications Group for just under a month. After three days away from the office, you find the following items in your in-basket:

- a memo from Bill Richards to Rena Morgan, concerning a new training course
- a memo from Bill Richards to you, concerning his workload
- a memo from Sandra Fineberg to you, concerning Bill Richards

READ THE IN-BASKET MATERIALS WHICH FOLLOW.

IN-BASKET ITEM ONE
MEMORANDUM

TO: Rena Morgan, Director, Bureau of Communications
FROM: Bill Richards
SUBJECT: What this Department needs . . .

> **TO:** You
>
> *What is this about?*
> *Rena*

. . . is a new training course on "Ethical Decision Making."

From my experience in working with public inquiries and Department correspondence, it strikes me that our decisions are difficult, and the "best" solutions are seldom without costs. Yet we need to make these decisions without undue delay.

In one of my graduate courses, we studied F. Mosher, who emphasized the need for flexibility and value priorities in public decision-making. There is a high ethical content in governmental decisions - often they do not succumb neatly to factual analysis. Rarely are they totally right or totally wrong. And the public character of this Department's decisions adds complicating dimensions to ethical behavior.

Anyway, I have lots of ideas that would be useful for this course. I'd like to present it to interested Department employees in general and bureau staff in particular (they need it!).

I'm available to discuss this in further detail, at your convenience.

IN-BASKET ITEM TWO
MEMORANDUM

TO: You, Head, Central Communications Group
FROM: Bill Richards
SUBJECT: Workload

I am pleased to be assigned to this group, since the work involves critical activities occurring throughout the Department. I enjoy most of the work I have had to date, and am always eager for more.

However, I get the impression that you think some of my work is "incomplete" or has "erroneous" information. Let me point out that I probably produce more than Frank's and Mary's units combined. Maybe if they did more of their share of the work I would feel less rushed.

So far all of my assignments involve gathering information or preparing letters or reports under very tight deadlines. I would like to get some assignments that involve longer range planning or project development as well as get a chance to do some public speaking. Also, there are some divisions I am not familiar with. If I knew more about the work of these divisions, I'm sure my work would be even better.

I would appreciate the opportunity to discuss better ways of scheduling the workload with you as soon as possible. I had a course in workload scheduling if that will be of any help.

IN-BASKET ITEM THREE
MEMORANDUM

TO: You, Head, Central Communications Group
FROM: Sandra Fineberg, Secretary 1

Bill Richards has insulted me again, and I feel it is just not fair. I must do work for four people in this group, but Bill insists that his work is "top priority" and should be done first. He told me I am just too slow!

I don't need this. I am going to request a transfer if the situation continues.

Continue now with SECTION A

SECTION A

To address the most urgent of these three memos, you would first deal with: **(Choose ONLY ONE.)**

1. Bill's memo and Rena's note about Bill's proposed training course
2. Bill's memo about the group's workload
3. Sandra's memo about Bill

- Mark '**A**' on your answer sheet if you are **selecting** that choice or action.
- Mark '**B**' on your answer sheet if you are **not selecting** that choice or action.
- You **must** mark **A or B** for **each** choice presented.

Then, go to SECTION B on the next page.

SECTION B

Rena calls you and expresses her concern about Bill Richards' manner in working with others. Rena comments that Bill produces a substantial amount of work, but it is not always accurate. Rena also says that she considers Bill abrasive and argumentative. She asks you to talk with Bill further and then get back to her.

You would now: **(Choose UP TO TWO.)**

4. Review available records of Bill's work performance and relationships.
5. Ask Frank and Mary if they have had any personal problems working with Bill.
6. Check informally with others in the Department and see how they view Bill.
7. Briefly review Frank's, Mary's, and Bill's unit assignments and overall workload.
8. Ask Sandra for a written list of the problems she has had with Bill.
9. Contact the director of the line division where Bill was employed for the last 18 months.

- Mark '**A**' on your answer sheet if you are **selecting** that choice or action.
- Mark '**B**' on your answer sheet if you are **not selecting** that choice or action.
- You **must** mark **A or B** for **each** choice presented.

This is the end of the Sample Background and Sections A and B.

The Solutions to Sections A and B are found on the following page.

Solution to Sections A and B from the Sample Job Simulation Exercise:

In the preceding sample Section A, the *most important* memo to address first is choice 3, and this choice is valued at +1. The memos described in choices 1 and 2 will require attention, but are not as critical as the urgent concerns expressed in Sandra Fineberg's memo (choice 3). Therefore, choices 1 and 2 are valued at 0.

Listed below are all the choices presented in sample Section A and their assigned values:

1. Bill's memo and Rena's note about Bill's proposed training course **0**
2. Bill's memo about the group's workload **0**
3. Sandra's memo about Bill **+1**

In the preceding sample Section B, the most helpful steps to take in gathering information before talking with Bill are described in choices 4 and 7. Choice 4 offers more comprehensive information on the quality and quantity of Bill's work performance and relationships, and choice 7 provides objective information about the distribution of work, which Bill views as a problem (see preceding memo). Therefore, in this "Choose UP TO TWO" section, choices 4 and 7 are valued at +1. Choices 5, 6, 8, and 9 are either less effective or inappropriate; therefore, these choices are valued at 0.

Listed below are all the choices presented in sample Section B and their assigned values:

4. Review available records of Bill's work performance and relationships. **+1**
5. Ask Frank and Mary if they have had any personal problems working with Bill. **0**
6. Check informally with others in the Department and see how they view Bill. **0**
7. Briefly review Frank's, Mary's, and Bill's unit assignments and overall workload. **+1**
8. Ask Sandra for a written list of the problems she has had with Bill. **0**
9. Contact the director of the line division where Bill was employed for the last 18 months. **0**

Scoring Sections A and B from the Sample Job Simulation Exercise:

Section A is a **"Choose ONLY ONE"** section. There is only **one** positive choice in this section, choice 3, and that choice is valued at +1. There are two other choices in this section, choices 1 and 2, and they are valued at 0.

In a "Choose ONLY ONE" section, only one of the candidate's choices is scored. A choice with a value of 0 is scored before a choice with a value of +1.

- A candidate would receive the maximum credit for this section (+1) if the choice valued at +1 was selected and none of the choices valued at 0 were selected (i.e., if the candidate marked 'A' on the answer sheet for choice 3 and 'B' for choices 1 and 2).
- A candidate would receive a section score of 0 if either of the choices valued at 0 were selected.
- If a candidate selected **more than** one choice, only one choice would be scored. A choice valued at 0 would be scored and additional choices valued at 0 or +1 would **not** be scored.
- A candidate would receive a section score of 0 if **no** choices were selected.

Section B is a **"Choose UP TO TWO"** section. There are **two** positive choices in this section, choices 4 and 7, which are valued at +1. There are four other choices in this section, choices 5, 6, 8, and 9, and they are valued at 0.

In a "Choose UP TO TWO" section, only two of the candidate's choices are scored. Choices with a value of 0 are scored before choices with a value of +1.

Some of the possible scoring outcomes include the following:

- A candidate would receive the maximum credit for this section (+2) if the two choices valued at +1 were selected and none of the choices valued at 0 were selected (i.e., if the candidate marked 'A' on the answer sheet for choices 4 and 7, and 'B' for choices 5, 6, 8, and 9.)

- A candidate who selected two choices, one valued at +1 and one valued at 0, would receive a section score of +1, the sum of the two choices.

- A candidate who selected *only one choice* would receive the score associated with that choice (i.e., either +1 or 0).

- If a candidate selected **more than** two choices, only two choices would be scored. The choices valued at 0 would be scored first, then the +1 choice, up to a maximum of two choices total.

- A candidate would receive a section score of 0 if **no** choices were selected.

End of Sample Job Simulation Exercise

MORE INFORMATION ON JOB SIMULATION EXERCISES:

Job simulation exercises present candidates with situational judgment problems, similar to those encountered on the job, and many possible answer choices.

Each answer choice is numbered. Candidates must select the best answer choice(s) presented and, on the separate scannable answer sheet, mark 'A' for the choice(s) selected and 'B' for the choice(s) not selected. Candidates must mark each and every answer choice as either one they are selecting or one they are **not** selecting.

In the preceding Sample Job Simulation Exercise, each choice has a value of +1 or 0. In sections that specify the number of choices to select (e.g. Choose ONLY ONE or Choose UP TO THREE), only that number of choices are scored. In these sections, a candidate's choices with a value of 0 are scored before the candidate's choices with a value of +1. If a candidate has selected more than the specified number, only the number of choices specified are scored.

To compute subtest scores for a job simulation exercise, candidate section scores are totaled and scaled according to the range of possible points for the subtest (e.g., 0 to 15, 0 to 30, etc.)

Directions for Job Simulation Exercises:

The job simulation exercises will present you with situations that are similar to those you might encounter on the job. The job simulation exercise will start with **Background** information that will tell you about the job setting and your role in that setting. The Background may also include some job-related issues, situations, and/or resource materials for you to consider.

You will then be given a series of situations in simulation Sections. Each Section will present the situation and choices representing possible responses one could make in that situation. You are to read the information and select the best choice(s) to take to collect relevant information and/or resolve the problem(s) in the situation presented.

The job simulation exercise will start with **Section A**. The Sections will continue in alphabetical order (Section B, then Section C, etc.) to the end of the exercise. Each Section will present you with choices, and you are to select the most appropriate choice(s) from among those presented.

Instructions for Selecting Answer Choices:

Each section will include an instruction on **how many** choices to select in that section. The instructions may tell you to:

- choose a specific number of choices, e.g., **"Choose ONLY ONE."**

- choose **"up to"** a maximum number of choices, e.g., **"Choose UP TO THREE."** (Candidates may choose fewer than three, but should not choose more than three.)

- choose as many choices as are appropriate, e.g., **"Choose AS MANY as are appropriate."**

Follow the instructions to each section carefully. Failure to follow the instructions may result in a lower score.

Instructions for Marking Answer Choices:

In order to be scored, all your answers must be recorded on a separate, scannable answer sheet. Using a No. 2 pencil, you are to mark 'A' for the choices you select and 'B' for the choices you are not selecting. The following instructions will appear at the end of each Section:

- Mark '**A**' on your answer sheet if you are **selecting** that choice or action.
- Mark '**B**' on your answer sheet if you are **not selecting** that choice or action.
- You **must** mark A **or** B for **each** choice presented.

You must mark either **A** or **B** for each choice presented because your answer sheet will be optically scanned by a machine that reads the darkest filled-in circle next to a choice number as your selection for that choice number. Marking **A** for choices you select and **B** for choices you do not select will ensure that your choices are recorded accurately.

Complete instructions on how to mark your answer sheet will be provided with your test materials on the day of your test. Be sure to follow these instructions carefully to ensure that your answers are scored correctly.

MENTAL DISORDERS AND TREATMENT PRACTICES

This section reviews eight areas that are usually tested on examinations:

- The Characteristics of Various Psychiatric Disorders
- The Needs of Special Groups (Children, Geriatrics)
- The Influences of Environment, Society, and Family on Psychiatric Disorders
- Psychotropic Drugs (Reactions and Uses)
- The Assessment and Evaluation of Patients
- The Functions and Purposes of the Treatment Team
- The Development and Implementation of the Treatment Plan
- Methods for Handling People with Various Emotional or Psychiatric Disorders

THE CHARACTERISTICS OF VARIOUS PSYCHIATRIC DISORDERS

It is often difficult to assign labels to human behavior with any large degree of accuracy. Behavior sometimes changes rapidly, and the interpretation of what behavior a label actually represents can vary greatly from one person to the next. One can often learn a great deal more about a person by observing their behavior than by reading a diagnostic label about that person. Regardless, diagnostic labels can be helpful to members of a treatment team as a shorthand method of describing a group of behaviors one might expect from certain individuals. They are also required for many insurance forms. A diagnosis may be useful as long as one views the diagnosis as an ongoing process, and can continue to look at the patient with *new eyes*.

The Difference Between Neurosis and Psychosis

People suffering from a neurosis are usually able to manage with the concerns of daily life, although there is often some distortion in their concept of reality. Those suffering from a neurosis may feel inferior, unloved, or have a long-term feeling of fear or dread. They may have obsessions, compulsions or phobias, but they are rarely dangerous to themselves or others. They usually have some insight into their problems, and except in severe cases, don't require hospitalization. Many go through life without obtaining any help for their problems. Those who experience a psychosis, however, are out of touch with reality and live in an imaginary world. They may hear voices, feel that they are being persecuted, or experience very deep depressions. There is a very definite split between the reality of those suffering from psychoses and the reality of the world. Unlike those suffering from neuroses, those suffering from psychoses often lose track of time, person, and place, and they have little insight into the nature of their behavior. They usually require hospitalization and their behavior is sometimes injurious to other people or themselves, although they may insist that there is nothing wrong with them.

Categories of Neurosis

It is important to keep in mind that rarely will all of a patient's symptoms fall into any one category, and that symptoms may change over time from one category to another. *Anxiety Neuroses* constitute approximately 35% of all neurotic disorders. Those suffering from anxiety neuroses have a tendency to view the world as hostile and cruel, and may frequently restrict daily activities in order to feel safer in their environment. They often feel tense, worried, and anxious, but are unable to articulate exactly why they feel this way. Many anxious individuals are very uncertain of themselves in even minor stress producing situations, and they may have real difficulties in concentrating because of their high anxiety levels.

Other symptoms may include strong anxiety reactions with difficulty catching one's breath, perspiration, increased heart beat, dizziness, and feeling that they are dying. They may come to the Emergency Room of a hospital complaining of a heart attack or heart troubles. It is important to keep in mind that many elements of the anxiety reaction are seen in patients with other neurotic disorders.

Conversion Reactions or *Hysteria* involve the loss of ability to perform some physical function that the person could previously perform, which is psychogenic in origin. This reaction is an attempt by the individual to defend herself or himself from some anxiety producing situation by developing physical symptoms that have no organic or physical cause. These reactions are not common, and constitute less than five percent of neurotic disorders. The lost function is often symbolically related to a situation which has produced stress or anxiety, and is often an attempt to escape from that situation. The person may lose the ability to hear or speak, have unusual bodily sensations, or lose control of some motor function. Since there is no physical cause of dysfunction, some people assume that the pain or paralysis is not real, or that this type of person is faking. *Dissociative Reactions* also serve to protect the individual from particularly stressful situations. Amnesia, fugue, and multiple personalities are the major categories of dissociative reactions. Despite the prevalence of *amnesia* on soap operas, dissociative reactions account for less than five percent of all neurotic disorders. Amnesiacs usually forget specific information for a specified but variable period of time. The patient does not, however, forget his or her basic lifestyle or habits. In *fugue,* the person combines the amnesia with flight, and leaves the area where the stressful situation is. Usually the person is unaware of where he or she has been, or where he or she is going. There are very few cases of *multiple personalities.* In this disorder, the person shows different ways of responding to the environment. Each individual personality within the person is a complete personality system, and may dominate the person's reactions to his or her environment, depending upon the situation.

Obsessive-Compulsive Reactions involve either the inability to stop thinking about something the person does not want to think about, or the obligatory performance of a repetitive act. People experiencing these reactions often recognize they are irrational, but are unable to stop doing them. They often attempt to rearrange their environment, which they may perceive as threatening, in an attempt to impose control and structure, so they can control their environment and feel safer. Those suffering from compulsive reactions feel a strong need to perform or repeat certain behaviors, often in order to prevent something terrible from happening to them. (This might involve pre-determined ways to enter a room, brush their teeth, get into bed, begin conversations, etc.) Of course, many people may exhibit aspects of this behavior. Observing some professional baseball players before they pitch or take a pitch can certainly demonstrate this point. There is little cause for concern if the patterns are relatively temporary and help the person in some way obtain their goal. When the behaviors begin to unduly restrict a person's activities, then the situation becomes more serious. People exhibiting this behavior are often unable to make decisions effectively, are often perfectionists, have a strong need for structure, and are fairly rigid. Those who are obsessed with unwanted thoughts may have quite a variety of areas that they think about. The most common areas, however, concern religion, ethical concerns (something being absolutely right or wrong), bodily functions, and suicide.

Phobic Reactions involve a strong, persistent irrational fear of an object, condition, or place. It is believed that phobias usually involve a displacement of anxiety from the original cause to the phobic object. The phobia serves to assist the individual in avoiding the anxiety-causing situation. Some of the most common phobias include fear of crowds, being alone, darkness, thunderstorms, and high places. It is often very difficult to discover the symbolic significance of a particular phobia.

Neurotic Depressive Reactions involve an intensification of normal grief reactions. Research has indicated that those suffering from this reaction are unable to *bounce back* from upsetting or discouraging events. People who suffer from this reaction tend to have a poor self-concept, exaggerated dependency needs, a tendency to feel guilty about almost anything, and to turn those guilt feelings against themselves in a highly punitive way. The possibility of suicide should be kept in mind when working with these patients.

Categories of Psychosis

Psychoses are generally divided into two categories, *functional psychoses* and *organic psychoses*. Functional psychoses are caused by psychological stress, while organic psychoses are caused by a disorder of the brain for which physical pathology can be demonstrated. A third category, *toxic psychoses,* is sometimes used to refer to psychotic reactions caused by toxic substances such as drugs or poisons.

Schizophrenia accounts for approximately 25 percent of all first admissions to mental institutions, and is the largest single diagnostic group of psychotic patients. The *paranoid schizophrenic* shows a great deal of suspiciousness and hostility, and may be very aggressive. The *simple type schizophrenic* is shy and withdrawn, and shows interest in his or her environment. The *hebephrenic schizophrenic* often has bizarre mannerisms and may appear quite manic. He or she may laugh and giggle inappropriately, and become preoccupied with unimportant matters. The *catatonic schizophrenic* may remain motionless for days or hours, and may refuse to eat. The two phases of catatonia are the *stuporous phase* where the person is motionless and *catatonic excitement* where the person is over-active and appears manic. While the catatonic schizophrenic may alternate between these two phases, most show a preference for just one. Someone suffering from *schizoaffective schizophrenia* will have significant thought disorders and mood variations. They may initially appear to be depressed or manic, but a basic personality disorganization also exists. These are the major categories of schizophrenia you should need for the exam. Since the exam announcement states basic knowledge is required, it is very possible some of the above categories may be too specific. We have included them just in case, however.

The general symptoms of schizophrenia include an inability to deal with reality, the presence of hallucinations or delusions, inappropriate emotions, autism and various other unusual behaviors. There is often a very noticeable inability to organize thoughts. Schizophrenic reactions that occur suddenly are referred to as *acute* schizophrenic reactions, while those that develop slowly over a rather lengthy period are called *chronic* schizophrenic reactions.

Paranoid Reactions in people account for less than one percent of psychiatric admissions. Those with this behavior usually mistrust the motives of everyone, are very resentful, and often hostile. They may show signs of grandiosity or persecution. The person often believes that whatever happens is related to him or her. The major difference between paranoid patients and paranoid schizophrenics is that the paranoid patient usually has better control of his or her thought processes, and is able to make more appropriate responses to situations. They are usually more reality-oriented, and able to state their feelings more effectively.

Affective Reactions are those that represent a change in the normal affect, or mood, of a person. There are two major categories of affective disorders: *manic-depressive reactions* and *involutional psychotic reactions.* In the manic-depressive reaction, the manic and depressive states alternate. In the manic phase, the person may be extremely talkative, agitated or elated, and demonstrate a great deal of physical and verbal activity. They may also exhibit some grandiosity. In the depressive phase, the person is joyless, quiet, and inhibited. The manic reactions are often divided into three degress of severity, each category representing a more severe degree of manic reaction. *Hypomania* is the least severe, *acute mania* is the next, and *delirious mania* is the most severe state. The term *involutional psychosis is* usually related to a patient's age. For women, the involutional age is considered to be somewhere between 40 and 55, and the involutional period for men is somewhere between 50 and 65. It seems that stresses are greater for men and women during these periods, and that these stresses may trigger psychotic reactions which are generally transient. These people generally have a long history of feeling guilty and very anxious, have little diversity of activity, and few sources of satisfaction in their lives.

Selected Personality Disorders

This category includes behavior which is maladaptive, but neither psychotic nor neurotic. This group includes *antisocial reactions,* the *abuse of alchol and other drugs,* and *sexual deviations*. The *antisocial* or *sociopathic* personality type fails to develop a concern for others and uses relationships to get what he or she wants. There is little or no concern about what effect their behavior might have on others, and they seldom feel remorse or guilt. They are often likable, friendly, intelligent people. Their relationships with others tend to be superficial, however, because they lack the capacity for deep emotional responses. The sociopath is often impulsive and seeks immediate gratification of his or her wants. He or she often is unreliable, untruthful, undependable and insincere. A large number of people have sociopathic traits which, as with most other characteristics, vary in severity and number. Sociopaths are found in all professions, although many are able to control their acting out behaviors or channel them in more socially acceptable ways. They avoid acting out not because of internal values, but because they do not wish to get caught. Sociopaths usually have a low frustration tolerance, are easily bored, and continually seek excitement. The sociopath most frequently comes to treatment because he or she has been *caught* doing something or been required to seek help by an employer or family member.

Sexual Deviations occur in those who fail to develop what their society considers appropriate sexual behavior. The major sexual deviations include child molestation, rape, sadism, masochism, voyeurism, fetishism, transvestism, exhibitionism, pedophilia, and incest. As you can see, some of these behaviors are much more harmful to other people than others are.

PSYCHOTROPIC DRUGS (REACTIONS AND USES)

The two major classifications of the psychotropic drugs are the tranquilizers, which are further divided into major (or anti-psychotic) and minor (or antianxiety) groups, and the antidepressants. Other drugs used include anticonvulsants, sedatives, hypnotics, and antiparkinsons.

Tranquilizers are meant to calm disturbed patients, and free them from agitation or disturbance. Drugs designed as *antipsychotic,* or *major tranquilizers,* also help to reduce the frequency of hallucinations, delusions, thought disorders, and the type of withdrawal seen in catatonic schizophrenia. It may take several days of drug therapy before the symptoms begin to subside, but during this time the patient becomes less fearful, hostile and upset by his disturbed sensory perceptions. The *phenothiazine derivatives* are the largest group of antipsychotic drugs. All the drugs in this group have essentially the same type of action on the body, but vary according to strength and the type and severity of their side effects. These drugs include:

Thorazine	Trilafon	Taractan
Mellaril	Compazine	Navane
Stelazine	Dartal	Sordinal
Prolixin	Proketazine	Haldol
Sparine	Tindal	Loxitane
Vesprin	Repoise	Moban

Serious side effects are very important to watch for. For these drugs, the phenothiazine derivatives, there are three major types of extrapyramidal symptoms (EPS): (1) akinesia - inability to sit still, complaints of fatigue and weakness, and continuous movement of the hands, mouth, and body; (2) pseudoparkinsonism -restlessness, mask-like facial expressions, drooling, and tremors; (3) tardive dyskenesia - lack of control over voluntary movements. Symptoms may include involuntary grimacing, sucking and chewing movements, pursing of the tongue and mouth, jerking of the hands, feet and neck, and drooping head. Immediate action must be taken to combat these side effects. The administration of antiparkinson drugs usually produces a dramatic reduction in symptoms. Unless spotted and treated early, however, these can become permanent.

Other side effects may include muscle spasms, shuffling gait, skin rash, eye problems, trembling hands and fingers, fainting, wormlike tongue movements, sore throat and fever, yellowing of skin or eyes, dry mouth, constipation, excessive weight gain, edema, a drop in blood pressure when moving from a lying to standing position, decreased sexual interest, sensitivity to light and prone to sunburn and visual problems, blurred vision, drowsiness, and increased perspiration. Just about any physical symptom or behavior could be caused by a reaction to a drug.

Special Considerations: Patients receiving a high dose of a phenothiazine drug should have their blood pressure checked regularly. Long exposures of skin to sunlight should be avoided (a wide-brimmed hat and long-sleeved clothing can also help). If a patient receiving phenothiazines is lethargic and wants to sleep a great deal, the dose of the drug may be too high and need adjustment. Patients on phenothiazines should not drive or use dangerous equipment. These drugs greatly increase the effects of alcohol. In the first three to five days, a person may feel drowsy and dizzy upon standing. Antipsychotic drugs tend to mask the symptoms of diseases and dictate that patients receiving them undergo thorough physical examinations every six months.

The *Minor Tranquilizers,* or *antianxiety drugs,* reduce anxiety and muscle tension associated with it. They are useful primarily with psychoneurotic and psychosomatic disorders. When given in small doses, they are relatively safe and have few side effects. Unlike the antipsychotic drugs, some of the antianxiety drugs tend to be habit-forming. If the drug is discontinued, the person may experience severe withdrawal symptoms, such as convulsions or delirium. These drugs include:

Librium	Milpath	Frienquel
Azene	Deprol	Phobex
Tranxene	Milprem	Softran
Valium	Miltown	Atarax
Ativan	Robaxin	Vistaril
Serax	Solacen	Trancopal

Side effects may include rashes, chills, fever, nausea, headaches, poor muscle coordination, some inability to concentrate, and dizziness. Excessive amounts of these drugs may lead to coma and death; however, death is less likely with an overdose of minor tranquilizers than with an overdose of barbituates. Patients taking these should be cautioned against driving or performing tasks that require careful attention to detail and mental alertness.

Antidepressants, such as the *Tricyclic Antidepressants,* are used to elevate the patient's mood, and increase appetite and mental and physical alertness. Drugs in this group tend to take one to four weeks of use before significant changes occur in the patient's outlook. Since these drugs sometimes excite patients instead of sedating them, patients must be observed closely for reactions. These drugs include:

Elavil	Sinequan
Endep	Tofranil
Asendine	Aventyl
Morpramin	Vivactil
Adapin	Marplan
Presamine	Janimine

Common side effects include dry mouth, fatigue, weakness, nausea, increased appetite, increased perspiration, heartburn, and sensitivity to sunlight. *Serious side effects* include blurred vision, constipation, irregular heartbeat, problems urinating, headache, eye pain, fainting, hallucination, vomiting, unusually slow pulse, seizures, skin rash, sore throat and fever, and yellowing of eyes and skin.

Serious side effects include blurred vision, constipation, irregular heartbeat, problems urinating, headache, eye pain, fainting, hallucination, vomiting, unusually slow pulse, seizures, skin rash, sore throat and fever, and yellowing of eyes and skin.

Monoamineoxidose Inhibitors (MAO Inhibitors) are sometimes used for depression, but can have *very* serious side effects, and can also lead to serious hypertensive crisis. Their use must be very closely monitored. Their use with some over-the-counter drugs can be very serious. Foods containing Typtophen or Tyramine (some examples: caffeine, chocolate, herring, beans, chicken liver, cheese, beer, pickles, wine) should be avoided also. *Side effects* to watch for include severe headaches, stiff neck, nausea, vomiting, dilated pupils, and cold, clammy skin. A hypertensive crisis requires *immediate* treatment. These drugs include: Marplan, Nardil, Parnate, and Ludiomil.

In addition to the above psychotropic drugs, sedatives, hypnotics, anticonvulsants, and antiparkinsons drugs are also used. Since the exam announcement includes uses and reactions of only the psychotropic drugs, we will not review the non-psychotropic drugs. We will mention, however, the use and reactions of *Lithium Carbonate* (also known as Eskolith, Lithane,

Lithobid, and Lithonate). This drug is primarily used in the treatment of manic depressive psychoses since it is effective in decreasing excessive motor activity, talking, and unstable behavior by acting on the brain's metabolism. It also decreases swings in mood. The correct dose is close to the overdose level for this drug, so it is important to watch closely for symptoms and to report them immediately. *Common side effects* include dry mouth, metal taste, slightly increased urination, hand tremors, increased appetite, and fatigue. *Serious side effects* include greatly increased urination, nausea, vomiting, diarrhea, loss of muscle coordination, muscle cramps or weakness, irritability, confusion, slurred speech, blackout spells, and coma. These side effects require medical attention. *Special Considerations:* This drug must sometimes be taken from one to several weeks before the resident feels better. Hot weather, hot baths, and too much exercise can be dangerous, as too much perspiring can lead to an overdose. The person should drink two to three quarts of fluid a day, but should not drink large quantities of caffeine-containing beverages like coffee, tea, or colas.

GLOSSARY OF BASIC PSYCHIATRIC TERMS

TABLE OF CONTENTS

	Page
Accident Prone ... Anxiety	1
Anxiety Reaction (Anxiety Neurosis) ... Catatonic State	2
Character Disorder ... Conversion	3
Conversion Reaction ... Depression	4
Disorientation ... Environment	5
Epilepsy ... Free Association	6
Frustration ... Hypnosis (Hypnotic Trance)	7
Hypochondriasis ... Insight	8
Instinct ... Looseness of Association	9
Maladjustment ... Mind	10
Motivation ... Object	11
Obsession ... Paranoid State	12
Pathogenesis ... Projective Tests	13
Psyche ... Psychosomatic	14
Psychosurgery ... Reversal	15
Sadism ... Stress	16
Subject ... Turning Against the Self	17
Unconscious ... Waxy Flexibility	18

GLOSSARY OF BASIC PSYCHIATRIC TERMS

A

ACCIDENT PRONE
Special susceptibility to accidents due to psychological causes.

ADDICTION
A descriptive name for a type of psychiatric illness (character disorder) characterized by excessive psychological and/or physiologic dependence upon the intake of some substance, as, for example, alcohol or an opiate.

ADJUSTMENT
The series of technics or processes by which the individual strives to meet the continuous changes that take place within himself and in his environment. Synonym: adaptation. (Some authorities consider adjustment to refer particularly to psychological activity and adaptation to physiologic activity.)

AFFECT
Generalized feeling tone. (Usually considered to be more persistent than emotion and less so than mood.)

Affective, pertaining to affect.

Affective psychosis, a psychosis characterized by an extreme alteration in mood in the direction of mania or of depression.

AGGRESSION (Aggressive Drive)
A term used in various ways; in the usq.ge of psychiatry, an instinct-like force, much influenced by early experience, motivating the individual to destructive activity.

AIM
Intention or purpose; in psychiatric literature the term is used chiefly in the discussion of instincts; the *aim* of an instinctual drive may be defined as an action on the part of the individual that involves the *object* of the drive and results in gratification. Thus, the aim of the instinctual drive, hunger, is eating.

AMBIVALENCE
The experiencing of contradictory strivings or emotions toward an object or situation. In extreme form, characteristic of *schizophrenia.*

ANAL CHARACTER (PERSONALITY)
(1) In psychoanalysis a pattern of behavior in an adult that originates in the anal eroticism of infancy and is characterized by such traits as excessive orderliness, miserliness, and obstinacy.
(2) A type of character (personality) disorder in which many of the individual's conflicts and defenses remain those appropriate to the muscle-training period, usually characterized by such traits as parsimony, rigidity, and pedantry.

ANAL PERIOD
One of the developmental stages; the muscle-training period.

ANTHROPOLOGY
The science of man or mankind in the widest sense; the history of human society; the developmental aspects of man as a species.

ANXIETY
(1) Apprehension, the source of which is largely unknown or unrecognized. It is different from fear, which is the emotional response to a consciously recognized and usually external danger.
(2) A state of tension and distress akin to fear, but produced by the threatened loss of inner control rather than by an external danger.

Anxiety attack, a phenomenon characterized by intense feelings of anxiety plus such physiologic manifestations as increased pulse and respiratory rates and increased perspiration.

ANXIETY REACTION (ANXIETY NEUROSIS)

A *psychoneurosis* characterized by the more or less continuous presence of anxiety in excess of normal and occasional clear-cut *anxiety attacks.*

ATTITUDE

One's physical and emotional position and manner with respect to another person, thing, or situation.

Attitude therapy, a method of treatment utilizing the assumption by the personnel of attitudes calculated to exert a favorable effect upon the patient.

AUTISM

Self-preoccupation with loss of interest in and appreciation of other persons and socially accepted behavior. *Autistic thinking,* thought processes determined by inner needs and relatively uninfluenced by environmental considerations, a characteristic of *schizophrenia.*

AUTISTIC CHILD

In child psychiatry, a child who responds chiefly to inner thoughts who does not relate to his environment, and whose overall functioning is immature and often appears retarded.

B

BASIC DRIVE

In human psychology, one of a group of hereditarily transmitted motivating forces, deriving ultimately from biochemical changes within the organism; used synonymously with instinct.

BEHAVIOR (HUMAN)

All the activity of a human being that is capable of observation by another person.

BEHAVIOR DISORDER

See Personality Disorder.

BLOCKING
- (1) Difficulty in recollection, or interruption of a train of thought or speech, caused by unconscious emotional factors.
- (2) An involuntary, functional interference with a person's thinking, memory or communication. (Usually the term is employed with reference to a psychotherapeutic situation.)

C

CASTRATION

Literally, the removal or the destruction of the gonads (ovaries or testes). In psychoanalytic terminology, the loss of the penis.

CASTRATION ANXIETY

Anxiety due to danger (fantasied) of loss of the genitals or injuries to them. May be precipitated by everyday events that have symbolic significance and appear to be threatening, such as loss of job, loss of a tooth, or an experience of ricidule or humiliation.

CATALEPSY

A condition usually characterized by trance-like states. May occur in organic or psychological disorders or under hypnosis.

CATATONIC STATE (Catatonia)
- (1) A state characterized by immobility with, muscular rigidity or inflexibility and at times by excitability. Virtually always a symptom of schizophrenia.
- (2) One of the four classic schizophrenic subgroups (syndromes), usually beginning at a

relatively early age and characterized by a rapid onset and interference with normal motor function.

CHARACTER DISORDER
See Personality Disorder.

COMPENSATION
(1) A defense mechanism, operating unconsciously, by which the individual attempts to make up for (i.e., to compensate for) real or fancied deficiencies.
(2) A conscious process in which the individual strives to make up for real or imagined defects in such areas as physique, performance, skills, or psychological attributes.

COMPLEX
(1) A group of associated ideas that have a common emotional tie. These are largely unconscious and significantly influence attitudes and associations. Examples are:

Inferiority Complex - Feelings of inferiority stemming from real or imagined physical or social inadequacies that may cause anxiety or other adverse reactions. The individual may overcompensate by excessive ambition or by the development of special skills, often in the very field in which he was originally handicapped.

Oedipus Complex - Attachment of the child for the parent of the opposite sex, accompanied by envious and aggressive feelings toward the parent of the same sex. These feelings are largely repressed (i.e., made unconscious) because of the fear of displeasure or punishment by the parent of the same sex. In its original use, the term applied only to the male child.

(2) In psychoanalytic terminology, a group of associated ideas and feelings that, though unconscious, influence the subject's conscious attitudes and behavior.

COMPULSION
(1) An insistent, repetitive, and unwanted urge to perform an act that is contrary to the person's ordinary conscious wishes or standards. Failure to perform the compulsive act results in overt anxiety.
(2) An act that is carried out, in some degree, against the subject's conscious wishes, either to avoid the anxiety that would otherwise appear, or to dispel a disturbing *obsession*.
compulsive, pertaining to a compulsion.

COMPULSIVE PERSONALITY
A type of personality disorder; more specifically, a type of neurotic personality. *See* Anal Character (Personality).

CONFLICT
A struggle between two or more opposing forces. *Intrapersonal* (*intrapsychic; conflict,* a struggle between forces within a single personality. *Interpersonal conflict,* a struggle between two or more individuals.

CONGENITAL
Present from birth; mayor may not be hereditary.

CONSCIENCE
Equivalent to the conscious portion of the superego; in strict psychoanalytic terminology, the "ego ideal."

CONSCIOUS
Aware or sensible; "mentally awake."

CONVERSION
Sensory or motor dysfunctions by which the subject gives symbolic expression to a conflict (of which he is not conscious).

CONVERSION REACTION
A psychoneurosis, formerly called "conversion hysteria," characterized by conversions.
CULTURE
The characteristic attainments of a people.
CYCLOTHYMIA
A tendency or a proneness to repeated, exaggerated, largely irrational alterations in mood, usually between euphoria and depression.

Cyclothymic, pertaining to cyclothymia.

Cyclothymia personality, a type of psychotic personality disorder, often the precursor of manic-depressive psychosis.

D

DEATH INSTINCT (Thanatos)
In Freudian theory, the unconscious drive toward dissolution and death. Coexists with and is in opposition to the life instinct (Eros).
DEFENSE MECHANISM
(1) A specific process, operating unconsciously, that is employed to seek relief from emotional conflict and freedom from anxiety.
(2) A psychological technic performed by the ego but carried out below the subject's threshold of awareness, designed to ward off anxiety or unpleasant tensions.

DELIRIUM
An altered level of consciousness (awareness), often acute and in most instances reversible, manifested by disorientation and confusion and induced by an interference with the metabolic processes of the neurons of the brain. *Delirium tremens,* an agitated delirious state occurring as a complication of chronic alcoholism.

DELUSION
A fixed idea, arising out of the subject's inner needs and contrary to the observed facts as these are interpreted by normal persons under the same circumstances; a symptom of psychosis.

DEMENTIA
A chronic, typically irreversible deterioration of intellectual capacities, due to organic disease of the brain that has produced structural changes (the actual death of neurons).

Dementia paralytica, formerly "paresis," a chronic syphilitic inflammation of the brain and its membranous coverings resulting, if untreated, in progressive dementia and paralysis and ultimately in death.

Dementia praecox, an old (obsolescent) (and misleading) term for schizophrenia.

DENIAL
A *defense mechanism* in which the ego refuses to allow awareness of some aspect of reality.

DEPRESSION
(1) Psychiatrically, a morbid sadness, dejection, or melancholy; to be differentiated from grief, which is realistic and proportionate to what has been lost. A depression may be a symptom of any psychiatric disorder or may constitute its principal manifestation.
(2) A pathologic state brought on by feelings of loss and/or guilt and characterized by sadness and a lowering of self-esteem.

Neurotic depressive reaction, a state of depression of neurotic intensity in which *reality-testing* is largely unimpaired and in which physiologic disturbances, if present, are usually mild.

Psychotic depressive reaction, a state of depression of psychotic intensity in which reality-testing is severely impaired and in which physiologic disturbances *(vegetative signs)* are usually conspicuous.

Reactive depression, a state of depression -- intensity not specified -- for which the precipitating stress can be clearly discerned and seen to be of some magnitude.

DISORIENTATION

Confusion of the subject with respect to such information as the correct time and place, a knowledge of his personal identity and an understanding of his situation; typically seen in *delirium* and *dementia.*

DISPLACEMENT

A general term for a group of psychological phenomena (technics) in which certain strivings or feelings are (unconsciously) transferred from one object, activity, or situation to another (which acquires a similar meaning). The defense technic of sublimation is one example of a successful displacement.

DISSOCIATION

A breaking of psychic connections, of associations.

DISSOCIATIVE REACTION

Formerly called "hysterical amnesia." A psychoneurosis in which a group of thoughts, feelings and memories becomes separated from the rest of the personality.

DRIVE

See Basic Drive.

DYNAMIC (PSYCHODYNAMIC)

Pertaining to the forces operating within the personality and determining the behavior, particularly unconscious forces. Dynamic psychiatry, a psychiatry concerned with the understanding of such motivating forces.

E

EGO

(1) In psychoanalytic theory, one of the three major divisions of human personality, the others being the id and superego. The ego, commonly identified with consciousness of self, is the mental agent mediating among three contending forces: the external demands of social pressure or reality; the primitive instinctual demands arising from the id imbedded as it is in the deepest level of the unconscious; and the claims of the superego, born of parental and social prohibitions and functioning as an internal censor or "conscience."

(2) One of the three agencies or aspects of the mind, the ego is the aspect that is in contact with the environment through the sensory apparatus, that appraises environmental and inner changes and that directs behavior through its control of the motor apparatus.

ELECTROCONVULSIVE THERAPY (E.C.T., ELECTROSHOCK THERAPY)

A method of treatment of psychiatric disorders by passing an electric current through the brain, producing an artificial seizure.

ELECTROENCEPHALOGRAPH

An instrument, based on the string galvanometer, for measuring very small changes in potential derived from the electrical activity of the neurons of the brain. *Electroencephalogram,* the record obtained with the electroencephalograph, a "brain-wave tracing."

EMPATHY

(1) An objective awareness of the feelings, emotions, and behavior of another person. To be distinguished from sympathy, which is usually nonobjective and noncritical.

(2) A deep recognition of the significance of another person's behavior, which retains a certain objectivity and yet involves intellectual, emotional and motivational experiences corresponding to those of the other person.

ENVIRONMENT

All that surrounds the individual, including living and non-living, material and immaterial elements.

EPILEPSY

A disorder characterized by periodic seizures, and sometimes accompanied by a loss of consciousness. May be caused by organic or emotional disturbances.

Major epilepsy (grand mal) - Characterized by gross convulsive seizures, with loss of consciousness.

Minor epilepsy (petit mal) - Minor nonconvulsive epileptic seizures; may be limited to only momentary lapses of consciousness.

ETHOLOGY

The scientific study of the instincts. *Ethologist,* one who makes a scientific study of the instincts.

ETIOLOGY

Pertaining to causation; in medicine and nursing, pertaining to the causation of disease.

EUPHORIA

(1) An exaggerated feeling of physical and emotional well-being inconsonant with reality.
(2) An exaggerated (unrealistic) sense of well-being.

EXHIBITIONISM

Erotic pleasure in exposing the body to the view of others; in adults, a form of perversion when it is the principal form of erotic expression.

EXTROVERSION

A state in which attention and energies are largely directed outward from the self, as opposed to interest primarily directed toward the self, as in introversion.

F

FACULTY

A power or a function, especially a mental one.

FAMILY TRIANGLE

The situation, involving the child and the parents, in which the child experiences the wish to displace the parent of the same sex and possess the parent of the opposite sex. Family-triangle period, a developmental phase characterized by maximum intensity of these strivings. Synonymous with *Oedipal period.*

FANTASY (PHANTASY)

An image -- conscious or unconscious -- formed by recombinations of memories and interpretations of them.

FEAR

An experience, having both psychological and physiologic components, stimulated by the awareness of impending danger in the environment.

FIXATION

The persistence into later life of interests and behavior patterns appropriate to an earlier developmental phase.

FLATNESS OF AFFECT

A lack of normal emotional responsiveness, especially characteristic of *schizophrenia*.

FLIGHT OF IDEAS

A morbid type of thought sequence manifested through speech, characterized by its rapidity and by numerous and sudden shifts in topics, but that tends to be comprehensible to the normal observer. Typical of mania.

FREE ASSOCIATION

(1) In psychoanalytic therapy, spontaneous, uncensored verbalization by the patient of whatever comes to mind.

(2) A technic, used in *psychoanalysis,* in which the patient reports verbally his thoughts, emotions and sensations in whatever order they occur, making no effort at deliberate organization, censorship, or control.

FRUSTRATION

A blocking or nongratification of needs.

FUGUE

A major state of personality dissociation characterized by amnesia and actual physical flight from the immediate environment.

FUNCTIONAL

Pertaining solely or primarily to function. *Functional psychosis,* a psychosis occurring on the basis of disturbed mental functioning in the absence of structural brain damage.

G

GARRULOUSNESS

Excessive talkativeness, especially about trivial things.

GENITAL PHASE (OF DEVELOPMENT)

In psychoanalytic terminology, a synonym for emotional maturity.

GROUP

Any two or more persons who are set off from others, either temporarily or permanently, by a special type of association (relationship), as, for example, an important common interest.

Group therapy, a form of *psychotherapy* taking place among a group of patients under the guidance of a therapist.

H

HALLUCINATION

A sensory experience, occurring (in the absence of adequate reality-testing) on the basis of the subject's inner needs and independently of stimulation from the environment.

HALLUCINOGEN

A chemical substance capable of inducing hallucinations.

HEBEPHRENIA

One of the classic schizophrenic subgroups, the one having the most ominous prognosis. *Hebephrenic schizophrenia* is a synonym.

HEREDITARY

Genetically transmitted from parent to offspring.

HETEROSEXUAL

Pertaining to the opposite sex.

HOMEOSTASIS

A tendency to uniformity and stability in the normal body states of the organism (Walter B. Cannon).

HOMOSEXUAL

(adj.) Pertaining to an erotic interest in members of one's own sex. (noun) One having an erotic interest in members of his own sex.

(1) Sexual attraction or relationship between members of the same sex.

Latent homosexuality - A condition characterized by unconscious homosexual desires.

Overt homosexuality - Homosexuality that is consciously recognized or practiced.

(2) *Homosexuality,* a condition characterized by the subject's having an erotic interest in members of his own sex, a form of *personality disorder.*

HYPNOSIS (HYPNOTIC TRANCE)

(1) A state of increased receptivity to suggestion and direction, initially induced by the

influence of another person. The degree may vary from mild suggestibility to a trance state so profound as to be used in surgical operations.

(2) An artificially induced state, akin to sleep, in which the subject enters into so close a relationship with the hypnotist that the suggestions of the latter become virtually indistinguishable from the activity of his own ego.

HYPOCHONDRIASIS

(1) Overconcern with the state of physical or emotional health, accompanied by various bodily complaints without demonstrable organic pathology.

(2) A severe type of *psychoneurosis,* characterized by a morbid preoccupation with one's body and a partial withdrawal of interest from the environment. *Hypochondriac,* one afflicted with hypochondriasis.

HYSTERIA

A *psychoneurosis;* the older term for the conditions now designated as *conversion reaction* and *dissociative reaction.*

HYSTERICAL PERSONALITY

(1) A personality type characterized by shifting emotional feelings, susceptibility to suggestion, impulsive behavior, attention seeking, immaturity, and self-absorption; not necessarily disabling.

(2) A form of *personality disorder (neurotic personality)* characterized by conflicts and defenses similar to those found in persons with hysteria.
Hysteric, one afflicted with hysteria.

I

ID

The one of the three agencies or aspects of the mind that contains the psychic representations of the instinctual drives.

IDEATION

The process of forming ideas.

IDENTIFICATION

The adoption -- unconsciously -- of some of the characteristics of another person. Strictly speaking, the term refers to the result of the defense mechanism of *introjection.* (Sometimes identification and introjection are used loosely as synonyms.)

ILLUSION

A false perceptual experience occurring in response to an environmental stimulus; usually a symptom of serious mental illness.

INCEST

Culturally prohibited sexual relations between members of a family, usually persons closely related by blood, as father and daughter, mother and son, or brother and sister. INHIBITION

(1) Interference with or restriction of activities; the result of an unconscious defense against forbidden instinctual drives.

(2) The restraining or the stopping of a process; in psychiatry, the term usually refers to an inner force that opposes the gratification of a basic drive.

INSANITY

Now a term of legal or medicolegal significance only, referring to a mental disorder of sufficient gravity to bring the subject under special legal restrictions and immunities.

INSIGHT

(1) Self-understanding. A major goal of psychotherapy. The extent of the individual's understanding of the origin, nature, and mechanisms of his attitudes and behavior.

(2) In the broad psychiatric sense, the patient's knowledge that he suffers from an emo-

tional illness; in the narrow psychiatric sense, the patient's knowledge of the specific, hitherto unconscious, meaning of his symptom(s) or of some other aspect of illness.

INSTINCT

A term of many meanings; in dynamic psychiatric usage it is usually considered as synonymous with *basic drive.*

INSULIN COMA THERAPY

A method of treatment of psychoses through the induction of a series of comas by means of insulin injections.

INTERNALIZE

To place within (the mind). Said of a conflict or a state of tension that, in its original form, existed between an individual and some aspect of his environment, but that has come to exist within the mind (i.e., between one aspect of the personality and another). Thus *anxiety* is often found to be an *internalized fear.*

INTERPERSONAL

Existing between two or more individuals; often contrasted with intrapersonal.

INTERPRETATION

A scientific guess, made by a psychotherapist about a patient, explaining some aspect of the latter's thoughts, feelings or behavior.

INTRAPERSONAL (INTRAPSYCHIC)

Existing within a mind or a personality; often contrasted with *interpersonal.*

INTROJECTION

One of the *defense mechanisms;* the psychological process whereby a quality or an attribute of another person is taken into and made a part of the subject's personality (unconsciously). Often used loosely as synonymous with *identification.*

INVOLUTION (INVOLUTIONAL PERIOD)

A period in late middle age in which retrogressive physiologic changes take place, causing a loss of the capacity for reproduction. *Involutional psychosis,* a psychosis for which a major precipitating factor has been the advent of involution.

ISOLATION

One of the *defense mechanisms;* the psychological process whereby the actual facts of an experience are allowed to remain in consciousness, but the linkage between these facts and the related emotions or impulses is broken.

L

LATENCY (LATENCY PERIOD)

One of the phases of human development, occurring between the *family-triangle period* and *puberty* (approximately, ages 6 to 11 or 12 years), characterized by a relative instinctual quiescence coupled with a rapid intellectual development.

LEVELS OF AWARENESS (LEVELS OF CONSCIOUSNESS)

An expression referring to the fact that mental activity takes place with varying degrees of the subject's awareness: an individual may be entirely unaware, dimly aware, or fully aware of a given bit of mental activity.

LIBIDO

An inclusive term for the sexual-social drives.

LOBOTOMY (PREFRONTAL)

A psychosurgical procedure in which certain tracts of the brain are severed, thus stopping the interaction between the prefrontal areas (of the cerebral cortex) and the rest of the brain. Sometimes used as a therapeutic measure in severe psychoses.

LOOSENESS OF ASSOCIATION

A symptom of serious mental illness, usually of *schizophrenia,* in which the logical connections between a patient's successive thoughts are absent or are not discernible to the observer.

M

MALADJUSTMENT
A state of disequilibrium between the individual and his environment, in which his needs are not being gratified.

MALINGER
To feign an illness.

Malingerer, one who feigns an illness.

MANIA
(1) A suffix denoting a pathological preoccupation with some desire, idea, or activity; a morbid compulsion. Some frequently encountered manias are: *dipsomania,* compulsion to drink alcoholic beverages; *egomania,* pathological preoccupation with self; *kleptomania,* compulsion to steal; *megalomania,* pathological preoccupation with delusions of power or wealth; *monomania,* pathological preoccupation with one subject; *necromania,* pathological preoccupation with the dead; pyromania, morbid compulsion to set fires.

(2) A morbid state of extreme euphoria and excitement with loss of reality-testing; one of the phases of *manic-depressive psychosis.*

Manic (adj.), pertaining to mania; (noun), one who suffers from mania.

MANIC-DEPRESSIVE REACTION
A group of psychiatric disorders marked by conspicuous mood swings, ranging from normal to elation or to depression, or alternating. Officially regarded as a psychosis but may also exist in milder form.

Depressed phase - Characterized by depression of mood with retardation and inhibition of thinking and physical activity.

Manic phase - Characterized by depression of mood with retardation of thought, speech, and bodily motion, and by elation or grandiosity of mood, and irritability.

MASOCHISM
(1) Pleasure derived from undergoing physical or psychological pain inflicted by oneself or by others. It may be consciously sought or unconsciously arranged or invited. Present to some degree in all human relations and to greater degrees in all psychiatric disorders. It is the converse of sadism, in which pain is inflicted on another, and the two tend to coexist in the same individual.

(2) Finding gratification in pain; in the narrow sense, one of the perversions.

MASTURBATION
Erotic stimulation of one's external genitalia.

MATURITY
The state of being fully adult; psychologically characterized particularly by the ability to love others in a relatively non-selfish way.

MECHANISM (MENTAL, DEFENSE)
See Defense Mechanism.

MILIEU
The total environment, emotional as well as physical.

Milieu therapy, treatment by means of controlled modifications of the patient's environment.

MIND
The body in action as a unit. *Mental,* pertaining to mind as thus defined. *Mental illness,* accurately speaking, any illness of the mind, regardless of severity; often incorrectly restricted to severe psychiatric conditions.

MOTIVATION

A psychological state that incites to action.

MOURNING

The process that follows upon the loss of a love object, through which the subject gradually frees himself from the disequilibrium caused by the loss.

MULTIPLE PERSONALITY

A morbid condition, related to *dissociative reaction,* in which the normal organization of the personality is split up into distinct portions, all having a fairly complex organization of their own. (If there are only two such portions, the term dual personality is used.)

MUSCLE-TRAINING PERIOD

One of the developmental stages, lasting from the end of *infancy* to the beginning of the *family-triangle period* (about age 1½ to age 3), during which the child receives training in sphincter control and other motor activities. Synonymous with *anal period.*

MYELIN

The fatlike substance that forms a sheath around the medullated nerve fibers. *Myelinization,* the process of acquiring a myelin sheath.

N

NARCISSISM (NARCISM)

(1) Self-love, as opposed to object-love (love of another person). Some degree of narcissism is considered healthy and normal, but an excess interferes with relations with others.

(2) Self-love; extreme narcissism is the emotional position found in the newborn infant and in certain psychoses. The term is derived from the Greek legend of Narcissus, a youth who fell in love with his own image.

Narcissistic, loving oneself excessively in a childish or an infantile fashion.

NARCOSYNTHESIS

A form of psychiatric treatment in which contact is established with the patient while he is under the influence of a hypnotic drug.

NEGATIVISM

A tendency to resist suggestions or requests, often accompanied by a response that is, in some sense, the opposite of the one sought. *Negativistic,* expressing negativism.

NEOLOGISM

A newly coined word, or the act of coining such a word; a phenomenon seen in *schizophrenia* and in some cases of *organic brain disease.*

NEURASTHENIA

One of the psychoneuroses, related to *anxiety reaction,* characterized by chronic feelings of fatigue and tension and often by disturbances in the sexual function and minor disturbances in the digestive function.

NEUROPHYSIOLOGY

The physiology of the nervous sytem. *Neurophysiologist,* a specialist in neurophysiology.

NEUROSIS

See psychoneurosis.

O

OBJECT

A term with several meanings. In the broadest sense, it is used in contrast with the term *subject* and means anything in the environment, including another person. In a narrower sense, *object* refers to "a satisfying something" in the environment that is capable of offering instinctual gratification. Thus, *love object* refers to a person toward whom the subject experiences libidinal strivings.

OBSESSION
(1) Persistent, unwanted idea or impulse that cannot be eliminated by logic or reasoning.
(2) A thought, recognized by the subject as more or less irrational, that persistently recurs, despite the subject's conscious wish to avoid or ignore it.
obsessive, pertaining to or afflicted with obsessions.

OBSESSIVE-COMPULSIVE NEUROSIS
One of the psychoneuroses, characterized by *obsessions* and *compulsions* and an underlying personality type whose conflicts involve problems of the muscle-training period.

OEDIPUS
A character in Greek legend, who unwittingly killed his father and married his mother and was subsequently punished by the gods by being blinded. *Oedipus complex,* a term referring to the erotic attachment of the (normal as well as neurotic) small child to the parent of the opposite sex, repressed largely because of the fear of bodily mutilation ("castration") by the presumedly jealous parent of the same sex. *Oedipal period,* same as *family-triangle period.*

ORAL PERIOD
The first postuterine developmental period, roughly synonymous with infancy, in which the individual's central experiences are those involved in the act of sucking.

ORAL PERSONALITY
One of the *personality disorders,* characterized by the persistence in adult life of problems and defenses appropriate to the *oral period* of development.

ORGANIC
Based on structural alterations, gross or microscopic. *Organic psychosis,* a psychosis the etiology of which involves structural damage. (The term also includes *toxic psychosis,* in which the physical alterations are at a submicroscopic -- i.e., chemical -- level.)

ORGANISM
A general term for any living creature, including man.

OVERCOMPENSATION
A conscious or unconscious process in which a real or fancied physical or psychological deficit inspires exaggerated correction.

OVERT
Discernible; "out in the open."

P

PANIC (PANIC REACTION)
A morbid state characterized by extreme fear and/or anxiety, causing a temporary disorganization of the personality.

PARANOIA
Traditionally considered to be one of the three major functional (nonorganic) psychoses, but now generally thought to be one variety of paranoid schizophrenia. A pathologic state, characterized by extreme suspiciousness and highly organized delusions of persecution, occurring in the presence of a clear sensorium and relatively appropriate affective responses.

Paranoid, pertaining to paranoia or paranoid schizophrenia.

Paranoid reaction, an acute, often self-limited state, resembling paranoia; the term is inclusive of paranoid syndromes arising on the basis of organic disease.

PARANOID SCHIZOPHRENIA
One of the four major schizophrenic subgroups, characterized by the usual features of *schizophrenia* plus delusions of persecution and/or grandeur (often loosely organized), auditory hallucinations in keeping with the delusions, and a marked, generalized suspiciousness.

PARANOID STATE
Characterized by delusions of persecution. A paranoid state may be of short duration or

chronic.

PATHOGENESIS

The mode of development of disease states.

PERCEPTION

A psychological experience in which sensory stimuli are integrated to form an image (the significance of which is influenced by past experiences).

PERSONALITY

The whole group of adjustment technics and equipment that are characteristic for a given individual in meeting the various situations of life.

PERSONALITY DISORDER

In the limited (diagnostic) sense, a type of psychiatric illness in which the patient's inner difficulties are revealed, not by specific symptoms but by an unhealthy pattern of living. Thus used, roughly synonymous with *character disorder* and *behavior disorder.* In a broader sense, "disorder of the personality" is often used as equivalent to "mental illness" or "emotional illness:'

PERVERSION (SEXUAL PERVERSION)

A form of personality disorder, characterized by an alteration from the normal of the *aim* and/or the *object* of libidinal strivings. Examples: *sadism, masochism, voyeurism.*

PHANTASY

See fantasy.

PHOBIA

(1) An obsessive, unrealistic fear of an external object or situation. Some of the common phobias are *acrophobia,* fear of heights; *agoraphobia,* fear of open places; claustrophobia, fear of closed spaces; *mysophobia,* fear of dirt and germs; *xenophobia, fear* of *strangers.*

(2) The dread of an object, an act or a situation that is not realistically dangerous, but that has come to represent a danger.
Phobic, pertaining to phobias.

PHOBIC REACTION

One of the psychoneuroses, formerly called *anxiety hysteria,* characterized by the presence of phobias.

PRECONSCIOUS

One of the three levels of *awareness,* the quality attaching to an idea, a sensation or an emotion of which the subject is not spontaneously aware but can become aware with effort.

PREMORBID PERSONALITY

The status of an individual's personality (conflicts, defenses, strengths, weaknesses) before the onset of clinical illness.

PRIMARY GAIN

The adjustment (adaptational) value of a neurotic symptom per se.

PROJECTION

One of the *defense mechanisms,* a technic whereby feelings, wishes or attitudes, originating within the subject, are attributed by him to persons or other objects in his environment.

PROJECTIVE TESTS

(1) Psychological tests used as a diagnostic tool. Among the most common projective tests is the Rorschach (inkblot) test.

(2) A relatively unstructured, although standardized, psychological test in which the subject is called upon to respond with a minimum of intellectual restrictions, thereby revealing characteristic drives, defenses and attitudes. (Examples are the Rorschach and the Thematic Apperception Tests.)

PSYCHE
Actually synonymous with *mind;* frequently used in expressions suggesting a mind-body duality, as, for example, "psychosomatic," "psychophysiologic," and "psychic versus organic factors."

PSYCHIATRY
That branch of medicine that deals with the causes, the diagnosis, the treatment and the prevention of mental disorders.

Psychiatrist, a physician specializing in psychiatry.

Psychiatric nurse, a nurse specializing in the care of patients having mental disorders.

Psychiatric team, a group of professional and semiprofessional persons working together under the direction of a psychiatrist in the treatment of psychiatric, patients. (Usually the membership of such a team includes psychiatrist, psychiatric nurse, clinical psychologist, psychiatric social worker, occupational therapist, and psychiatric aide.)

PSYCHOANALYSIS
(1) A theory of human development and behavior, a method of research, and a system of psychotherapy, originally described by Sigmund Freud (1856-1939). Through analysis of free associations and interpretation of dreams, emotions and behavior are traced to the influence of repressed instinctual drives in the unconscious. Psychoanalytic treatment seeks to eliminate or diminish the undesirable effects of unconscious conflicts by making the patient aware of their existence, origin, and inappropriate expression.

(2) The term designates 1. a *method* of (a) psychotherapy and (b) psychological research, and 2. a body of *facts and theories* of human psychology. Both the method and the body of knowledge represent the work of Sigmund Freud and his followers. *Psychoanalyst,* a professional person, usually a physician, who has received specialized formal training in the theory and the practice of psychoanalysis.

PSYCHONEUROSIS (NEUROSIS)
(1) One of the two major categories of emotional illness, the other being the psychoses. It is usually less severe than a psychosis, with minimal loss of contact with reality.

(2) A mild to moderately severe illness of the personality (mind), in which the ego function of reality-testing is not gravely impaired, and in which the maladjustment to life is of a relatively limited nature.

Psychoneurotic, pertaining to or characteristic of a psychoneurosis.

PSYCHOPATHIC PERSONALITY
An older term for one of the varieties of *personality disorder,* roughly synonymous with the current (official) category of "sociopathic personality disturbance," a form of illness characterized by emotional immaturity, the use of short-term values and behavior that is asocial or antisocial.

PSYCHOSIS
(1) A major mental disorder of organic and/or emotional origin in which there is a departure from normal patterns of thinking, feeling, and acting. Commonly characterized by loss of contact with reality, distortion of perception, regressive behavior and attitudes, diminished control of elementary impulses and desires, and delusions and hallucinations. Chronic and generalized personality deterioration may occur. A majority of patients in public mental hospitals are psychotic.

(2) A very serious illness of the personality (mind), involving a major impairment of ego function, particularly with respect to reality-testing, and revealed by signs of a grave maladjustment to life.

Psychotic, pertaining to or afflicted with psychosis.

PSYCHOSOMATIC
Adjective to denote the constant and inseparable interdependence of the psyche (mind) and

the soma (body). Most commonly used to refer to illnesses in which the manifestations are primarily physical with at least a partial emotional cause.

PSYCHOSURGERY

A form of neurosurgery in which specific tracts or other limited portions of the brain are severed or destroyed with the intention of producing favorable effects upon the patient's psychological status.

PSYCHOTHERAPY

(1) The term for any type of mental treatment that is based primarily upon verbal or nonverbal communication with the patient in distinction to the use of drugs, surgery, or physical measures such as electric or insulin shock.

(2) A term with many shades of meaning. In the broadest sense it is equivalent to "psychological treatment measures;" in a narrower sense *psychotherapy* refers to a direct relationship between one or more patients and a professional person, the therapist, in which the latter endeavors "to provide new life experiences which can influence the patient in the direction of health" (Levine).

PSYCHOTIC PERSONALITY

A variety of personality disorder, synonymous with the current official term "personality pattern disturbance," in which, despite the absence of the usual clinical symptoms of psychosis, the individual's fundamental conflicts and defenses are those of a *psychotic.*

R

RATIONALIZATION

The process of constructing plausible reasons for one's responses (usually to avoid awareness of neurotic motives).

REACTION FORMATION

One of the *defense mechanisms,* a technic whereby an original attitude or set of feelings is replaced in consciousness by the opposite attitude or feelings.

REALITY-TESTING

The process of determining objective (usually external) reality, a function of the ego.

RECONSTITUTE

To form again. The term is used of a personality that, having become more or less disorganized through illness, resumes its previous defense measures and type of adjustment.

REGRESSION

(1) The partial or symbolic return to more infantile patterns of reacting.

(2) One of the *defense mechanisms;* a process in which the personality retraces developmental steps, moving backward to earlier interests, defenses, and modes of gratification.

REPRESSION

(1) A defense mechanisms, operating unconsciously, that banishes unacceptable ideas, emotions, or impulses from consciousness or that keeps out of consciousness what has never been conscious.

(2) One of the *defense mechanisms,* a technic whereby thoughts, emotions and/or sensations are thrust out of consciousness.

REVERSAL

One of the *defense mechanisms,* a technic whereby an instinctual impulse is seemingly turned into its opposite, as, for example, when *sadism* is replaced by *masochism.*

S

SADISM

A form of perversion characterized by the experiencing of erotic pleasure in inflicting pain on another person. Often used more broadly as meaning the enjoyment of cruelty. *(See Masochism.)*

SCHIZOID

Schizophrenic-like. *Schizoid personality,* a form of *personality disorder* (subgroup of *psychotic personality*) characterized by withdrawn, self-centered, often eccentric behavior.

SCHIZOPHRENIA

(1) A severe emotional disorder of psychotic depth, characteristically marked by a retreat from reality with delusion formation, hallucinations, emotional disharmony, and regressive behavior. Formerly called dementia praecox. Its prognosis has improved in recent years.

(2) One of the major *functional psychoses;* more accurately, a group of interrelated symptom syndromes, having in common a number of features, including *associative looseness, autistic thinking, ambivalence* and inappropriateness of *affect.* The classic subgroups are: *catatonic, paranoid, simple* and *hebephrenic* schizophrenia; other varieties are: *schizoaffective, undifferentiated, childhood* and *latent* schizophrenia. *Schizophrenic,* pertaining to or afflicted with schizophrenia.

SECONDARY GAIN

The adjustment value or gratification that occurs as a result of the way in which a patient's environment responds to his illness (not an integral part of the symptoms per se).

SELF-CONCEPT

A person's image of himself, usually his conscious image.

SENILE

Pertaining to (extreme) old age, particularly to the deterioration in adjustment capacity occurring in old age.

Senile psychosis, an organic psychosis resulting from the brain damage accompanying advanced age.

SHOCK TREATMENT

A form of psychiatric treatment in which electric current, insulin, or carbon dioxide is administered to the patient and results in a convulsive reaction to alter favorably the course of mental illness.

SIMPLE SCHIZOPHRENIA

One of the four classic *schizophrenia* subgroups, characterized by slow, insidious onset and chronic course, with the illness being shown by emotional coldness, withdrawal and eccentricity, rather than by more striking symptoms.

SOMATOPSYCHIC

A term of recent coinage, intended to indicate psychological effects of somatic pathology.

SPLIT PERSONALITY

A term calling attention to the schizophrenic's inappropriate-ness of affect; the "split" is thus between emotions and ideation.

STRESS

Any circumstance that taxes the adjustment capacity of the individual.

SUBJECT
The person under discussion or study, as, for example, a patient or a person upon whom an experiment is performed.

SUBLIMATION
(1) A defense mechanism, operating unconsciously, by which instinctual but consciously unacceptable drives are diverted into personally and socially acceptable channels.

(2) One of the *defense mechanisms,* the only one that is never pathogenic; a technic whereby the original aim or *object* of a basic drive is altered in a manner that allows the release of tension and, at the same time, is socially acceptable.

SUPEREGO
One of the three major aspects or agencies of the mind; similar to the term "conscience" but more inclusive since it involves both conscious and unconscious components. (*See* Ego.)

SUPPRESSION
A technic of adjustment -- differing from the *defense mechanisms* in that it is fully conscious and very rarely pathogenic -- whereby the ego denies expression to a thought or an impulse. (It is often contrasted with *repression,* which is automatic, unconsciously effected and frequently pathogenic.)

SYMBOLISM
The use of one mental image to represent another.

T

TOXIC
Pertaining to, or due to the action of, a poison.

Toxic psychosis, a psychosis brought about by the action of a poisonous substance or, more broadly, a psychosis brought about by any chemical interference with normal metabolic processes (grouped with the *organic psychoses*).

TRANSFERENCE
The attributing by the subject, to a figure in his current environment, of characteristics first encountered in some figure of his early life, and the experiencing of desires, fears, and other attitudes toward the current figure that originated in the relationship with the past figure. The term is most commonly used with respect to feelings of a patient toward his therapist.

Counter-transference, transference feelings of a therapist toward his patient.

TRAUMA
Harm or injury; sometimes, the circumstances productive of harm or injury. In psychiatry, the term is inclusive of purely emotional as well as physical injury.

Traumatic, harmful, pertaining to trauma.

TRAUMATIC NEUROSIS (WAR NEUROSIS)
An acute morbid reaction related to *psychoneurosis* but occurring only in response to overwhelming trauma or stress. The condition is characterized by a temporary, partial disorganization of the personality, followed by such symptoms as anxiety, restlessness, irritability, impaired concentration, evidence of autonomic dysfunction and repetitive nightmares in which the traumatic experience is "relived."

TURNING AGAINST THE SELF
One of the *defense mechanisms,* a technic in which an unacceptable drive (usually aggressive) is diverted from its original object and (unconsciously) made to operate against the self, in whole or in part.

U

UNCONSCIOUS
(1) That part of the mind the content of which is only rarely subject to awareness. It is the repository for knowledge that has never been conscious or that may have been conscious briefly and was then repressed.
(2) In psychiatry, one of the three *levels* of *awareness;* thoughts, sensations, and emotions at this level cannot enter the subject's awareness through any voluntary effort on his part, but they continue to exert effects upon his behavior.

UNDOING
One of the *defense mechanisms,* a technic in which a specific action is performed that is (unconsciously) considered by the subject to be in some sense the opposite of a previous unacceptable action (or wish), and thus to neutralize ("undo") the original action.

V

VEGETATIVE SIGNS (OF DEPRESSION)
A traditionally grouped set of findings, including anorexia, weight loss, constipation, amenorrhea, insomnia and "morning-evening variation in mood," that, when found in combination, are indicative of severe depression.

VOYEURISM
A form of *personality disorder* (more specifically, of *perversion*), in which the subject receives his principal erotic gratification in clandestine peeping.

W

WAXY FLEXIBILITY
A phenomenon, associated with *catatonic schizophrenia,* in which the body, particularly the extremities, will remain for long periods of time in any positions selected by the examiner.